Common Cause

Common Cause

Francis Combes
Translated by Alan Dent

STACK
BOOKS

Published 2010 by
Smokestack Books
PO Box 408, Middlesbrough TS5 6WA
e-mail : info@smokestack-books.co.uk
www.smokestack-books.co.uk

Common Cause
Francis Combes

Cover image, *Les Maquis de France* by
Jean Amblard (Ville de Saint-Denis)

Printed by
EPW Print & Design Ltd

ISBN 978-0-9560341-8-2
Smokestack Books gratefully
acknowledges the support of
Arts Council England

LOTTERY FUNDED

Middlesbrough
moving forward

Smokestack Books is
represented by Inpress Ltd
www.inpressbooks.co.uk

Contents

Preface

Three things I want to say about this work, which Francis Combes began writing after the fall of the Berlin Wall and the collapse of the Soviet Union in 1989, and which he continued to work on until the year 2000. A decade's work.

1 – I've never seen another book like it. It's poetry, it's a thesis about history, it's a roll-call of revolutionary martyrs during two or three millennia, it includes many jokes, it's an intimate confession – not of an individual penitent, but of the wounded body of a set of political beliefs, it's a prayer book of hopes, and, finally, it's a chapbook, like those once sold by pedlars. Yet, despite its startling originality, *Cause Commune* is in no way eccentric or obscure. As soon as it's in your hands, you recognize it. It's a book that innumerable people have been waiting to read. It'll be passed, I think, from hand to hand.

2 – I remember this book (because I read it a while ago, in French and, yes, the translations are excellent). I remember it and will remember it not only as a volume of 350 pages but also as a place. This is because it's an assembly point where men and women, who never physically met, nevertheless come together.

In Combes' poems the prophet Isaiah and Democritus belong to the same confraternity. Rosa Luxemburg becomes contiguous with the Irish martyr Bobby Sands. Picasso listens to the replies of Socrates. Lenin faces Marat. Pol Pot is judged by the same jury as Stalin. Combes talks to Bertolt Brecht. Babeuf is welcomed by the Spanish Republicans. It is also a confraternity of the anonymous, all of whom had their nicknames. The place is an assembly point but it's more than this. It's the place prisoners in their cells see when they shut their eyes, the imagined place which gives strength to women and men and kids when they decide, whatever the risk, to resist, the place that the condemned fix their eyes on, before being executed. It's a place that encourages great modesty, the place of hope glimpsed by all those who actively resist injustice. There are many doors to it. Francis Combes as poet had the key to one of them.

3 – the chapbook, the pages, the place have a distinct voice. A voice with many registers – sometimes didactic, sometimes sardonic, sometimes furious, sometimes tearful, sometimes wondrous. Yet whatever the register, the voice remains itself. A voice that has no luggage and is not in a hurry. Listening to it, you can't tell whether, outside, it's night or day. A voice that comes from nowhere in particular and, at the same time, is much travelled. An open voice – ready to listen, and to question. A voice that has no love for conclusions. The voice of endurance. An endurance which is not heavy and passive but supple and active – just as its words are active. Active concerning the unfinished past, the ever-present and the future which the present secretly contains. A voice which accompanies us in our endless struggle. As the first poem says:

'This is the history of a great dream which betrayed hope
But the victory gained over this dream
is a victory without hope.
This is a history to read in the catacombs
an ancient history
which comes from places remoter than ourselves and which
    will go further.'

John Berger, Quincy, France

Introduction

Marx is reputed to have written, in a letter to Edward Spencer Beesly in 1869: 'The man who draws up a programme for the future is a reactionary.' Perhaps a surprising formulation for the author the *Communist Manifesto,* but a wise word of warning. The ancient communist hankering, the impulse towards a society of equality, peace, individual freedom through collective means, has given rise to a plethora of blueprints and the societies calling themselves communist have been authoritarian, grossly unequal, totalitarian, nightmarish. Yet the hankering persists as does the theorizing and the activism. Where does it come from then, this sense that a radically different form of society is possible? And different from what? We have thousands of years of evidence to suggest humanity celebrates hierarchy, worships power, relishes brutality, glories in war, disdains the notion of egalitarian communalism. Curiously, one of the most telling defences of socialism comes from an intellectual who briefly stepped out of his expertise in the mid twentieth century. Bringing to bear the objectivity common to his science, Einstein argued that the relation of the individual to society is the pressing problem of modern times:

> 'The individual has become more conscious than ever of his dependence on society. But he does not experience this dependence as a positive asset, as an organic tie, as a protective force, but rather as a threat to his natural rights, or even to his economic existence. Moreover, his position in society is such that the egotistical drives of his make-up are constantly being accentuated, while his social drives, which are by nature weaker, progressively deteriorate.'

The social nature of individuality is no more obvious than the status of energy and matter. Our experience tells us we are individuals and this powerful sense of autonomous identity easily leads us astray or is exploited. Our identity seems so intrinsic, so indefeasible, it's hard to accept it depends on formations and that outside society, ceases to exist. We are born to become unique individuals just as we are born to be linguistic, but we don't learn to speak without a linguistic community. Language, as Darwin astutely put it, is 'an instinct to acquire an art'. So is identity. The social theorists, the utopians, the dreamers, the anarchists, that long pedigree of miscellaneous proponents of a new world who inspired or appalled the so-called scientific thinkers, were searching for the clue to how identity is created. Like Darwin who could see how natural selection worked, they spotted patterns in history: people's idea, values, behaviour are closely tied to the forms of society they inhabit; but like Darwin too, they didn't know the mechanism. Slowly, it's starting to come into focus.

In her extraordinary book *Friday's Footprint: How Society Shapes The Human Mind,* Leslie Brothers includes this innocuous observation: 'Social stimuli have physical effects on neurons.' The social stimuli and the physical effects are always precise. Not only does the precise social context in which you grow and live shape your ideas, your values, your behaviour, your emotions, it changes the shape of your brain. Brothers is very insistent that mind can't be reduced to brain: it's culture that makes mind; but it does so very precisely. We aren't what we are intrinsically, we are what we are in circumstances and only in circumstances. Our genetic inheritance is a mere beginning.

Consider this example: it's estimated that a child growing in a linguistically enriched environment hears, by school age, thirty-two million more words than a child growing in linguistic impoverishment. All those words are processed by precise neurons. By the time children start school, those from the advantaged backgrounds have far better developed linguistic brains. Further, they are likely to go to school with other children from the same kind of background, while those who are disadvantaged will do the same. How can the school compensate? Because we allow our societies to divide into havens of privilege and ghettoes of deprivation, before their lives have barely begun millions of children have suffered disadvantage they will probably never overcome. We celebrate this as a culture of opportunity only because we fail to understand the damage.

Einstein's insight that society has become a threat to individuals is the most powerful argument for a reworking of our social and economic arrangements to remove what he calls the crippling of individuals. If the crippling were obvious, if the poor all had rickets, or terrible deformities, or skin diseases, we would act; but the crippling is to identity so we can claim it's nothing to do with us. It's the way some people are. Yet it isn't the poor alone who are crippled by modern society, the rich become victims of their own system and, hollowed out, believe in their own propaganda so thoroughly they bring the system in which they believe to the edge of collapse. Humanity creates and replicates the conditions of its own dehumanization. The need for change is urgent.

> 'All human beings, whatever their position in society, are suffering from this process of deterioration. Unknowingly prisoners of their own egotism, they feel insecure, lonely, and deprived of the naïve, simple, and unsophisticated enjoyment of life. Man can find meaning in life, short and perilous as it is, only through devoting himself to society.'

Mind is one hundred percent social. We are all born with a unique genetic endowment, but nothing can be made of it outside society. We don't learn to speak without others to hear and speak to. Imagine an individual with Mozart's musical potential born five thousand years ago. To write concertos you have to be part of a society where instruments have been refined, orchestras exist, a notation has been worked out. However great the contribution of individuals of genius, talent is worthless outside a social context which permits it to be realized. The pursuit of a new society, is the search for a new mind. Paramount is the need to overcome violence.

Francis Combes, in this erudite and fascinating poetic evocation of two centuries of the communist idea, frequently refers to revolution. More often than not, revolution is violent but to commit an act of violence is to be wrong about your human status; just as we were wrong in thinking the earth keeps the sun in its orbit or that species arrived one after another in a stately hierarchy. On what grounds can anyone claim they have a right to do violence to others? Violence is an assertion of superiority. It is a claim that the life of the perpetrator is more valuable than that of the victim. How can a hierarchy of value be attributed to human lives? We are all irrevocably inserted in our humanity. We can't step outside it to judge one life more valuable than another. All human lives are of equal value. That is the meaning of equality. Violence is the most fundamental assault on equality. If we are to establish a society in which every life is of equal value, violence must be renounced. Violence is easy to unleash and impossible to control. If there is to be revolution it must be by the most principled and fastidious means.

This book tells many stories which combine to bring to life the adventure of human history with all its joys, trials and tragedies. It is as far from the prevailing lyricism as a book of poetry could be because it never forgets that our individuality is socially engendered. In these two hundred poems Combes evokes the epic journey of an aspiration. The writing is clear but the nuances subtle and the picture complex. Some will try to dismiss it as propaganda but much more than serving a cause, Combes is trying to tease out a truth which it is difficult to hold in focus. Just as it's hard to remember all the time that gravity exists because large masses bend spacetime, so it's difficult to be conscious of the way the history we shape shapes us. Combes is fascinated by this fact. He relentlessly pursues its manifestations. He believes that to understand this is to illuminate part of the essential mystery of life. This is the great pleasure of this collection, its passionate impulse to be accurate about what it means to be human. But is the work weakened by taking sides? Literature can't be built out of journalistic tendentiousness but this is real literature because it doesn't seek to advance a ready-made view but to see from many angles a hard-won insight.

Einstein was right: alienation is the modern malaise. The cliché of capitalist societies is that they are built on the exploitation of labour by capital but the more telling recognition is that they are built on humanity's self-exploitation. When Lawrence wrote of 'things men have made with wakened hands' he was evoking work as self-realization. The simplest task, sweeping a floor or mending a chair, has the capacity to engage our imagination and to connect us to ourselves and others if we permit it, but when every task is reduced to the question of how much profit it can make, the creation of our best capacities rises against us as a monster of cold calculation. *Common Cause* is a contribution to what Murray Bookchin calls 're-enchanting humanity'. The tragedies of our brief occupation of the planet can't be erased, but the future gives us every day the chance to finally accept the truth of our human status and to shape a form of life based upon it.

Francis Combes is one of the movers behind the *Le Temps des Cerises* publishing house. He has written poetry, prose, drama and translated leading writers: Heine and Mayakovsky for example. *Cause Commune* is his most substantial collection to date. Written in his characteristic simple style it embraces a span of two thousand years. The poems tell stories, point up ironies, tell jokes, evoke tragedy. Combes is a unique voice in contemporary French poetry. He fits into no ready-made category or tradition. What marks his work most notably, is the almost complete absence of a dominating poetic persona. His subject is seldom himself. Rather, he ransacks history, literature, art. The retreat of the lyrical persona is in keeping with his conviction of the need for radical change. His work is an antidote to the narcissism so prevalent in the modern world. The energy and honesty of his writing make him in demand across the globe. He has read to audiences in China and San Francisco. Though some of Combes's work has been translated into English, this collection brings to English-speaking readers a major work by a unique voice. In a previous Smokestack collection *When The Metro is Free,* Combes appeared alongside Jacques Gaucheron, Françoise Coulmin, Georges Hassomeris and others. Combes is at the hub of a group of poets who stand outside the French mainstream and try to give voice to a questioning counter-culture. From his home in Aubervilliers his influence extends across the hexagon. He has established a cultural space which makes the Establishment uncomfortable. Determined not to give way to cynicism, convinced that language can gain purchase on reality, committed to the education of the emotions though art, Combes works in contradistinction to fashionable defeatism and compliance. The energy in *Common Cause* is pushing resolutely towards a more fundamental democracy, one that doesn't treat the workplace as beyond its reach. By searching the past two thousand years for examples, inspirations, lessons, ironies and illuminating defeats, Combes tries to open up a pathway to a future where, finally, we have learned to make ourselves at home in the world.

Alan Dent, Preston

Introït

This is the history of the defeated
the history of those whose history mustn't be told
This is the history of those whose names are wiped off the plaques
    on the streets as well as the pages of books
This is the history of those about whom we mustn't say
    they rose against the oppressor
the history of those about whom we must deny
    they tried to change the world
and sometimes succeeded
the history of those who not being resigned
must be thrown in dungeons
this is the secret history of the world
the history of the ideas which changed the world
and which the world has changed.
This is a history of ideas and of what men have
        made of them
a history of men and women, of their enthusiasm
        and their disillusions
This is a history of a human epic
with its heroes, its martyrs, its cowards, its executioners
        its saints, its inquisitions, its apostles, its traitors
        and its precursors
This is the epic of the unknown
and of those we thought we knew
the gestures of simple workers and peasants
of poets, of militants, of philosophers
a history of cries and tears
a history of roses and dust
a history of ice and burning sands
a history of reason and madness
of dignity and shame.

Because we have known the fable of the salt which lost its flavour
the wild river which disappears into the sands
the waves on the high seas which assault
        rocks then fall back and lick the feet
        of the bitter riverbank.

But we have known too
renewed dawns
Clearer mornings, generous harvests
and the flight of birds into the light
This is the history of an ancient dream never realised
*   but which never stops seeding the earth*
This is the epic of men's dreams
often disappointed but always being reborn
*   of a humanity at last reconciled to itself*
the long march of men towards their humanity
This is the history of a great dream which betrayed hope
But the victory gained over this dream
is a victory without hope.
This is a history to read in the catacombs
an ancient history
which comes from places remoter than ourselves and which will
*   go further.*

PROLOGUE

Questions about human nature

That man often displays a kindness
which costs his fellows dearly
(because he hesitates to fight his enemies) –
is that human nature?
That he often gives proof of remarkable
wickedness, which returns to haunt him
(because he agrees to serve his own enemies)
that he curses the vicissitudes of time
(about which he can't do much)
but remains silent before injustice,
that he cons the secrets of nature and commands the atoms
but can't command his own history –
is this in the nature of things?
That the majority lets itself be dominated by the minority
and that the progress of some
is at the cost of others' misery –
is this an immutable social law?
That in the course of his life the individual often
moves from the left to the right
and that revolutionaries having seized power
change into conservatives –
is this a product of eternal human nature?
So many theoretical questions
Which call for a practical answer.

The garden of Eden

Through all time, the goal was the same:
to live in a garden
where man would finally be a friend to man.
Every religion gave a name to this future not yet born
The Golden Age we must rediscover –
The Kingdom of God, the paradise of Allah, Eden
(or garden in Persian)
The Abbey Theleme, the Phalanstery, Icarie, the Future City,
The Kingdom of Freedom, the country of brotherhood,
Anarchy, Communism…
Through all time, the goal was the same
to reach the orchard in the valley,
behind the mountainous barrier blocking the horizon
an orchard where man would live in peace
with himself
and with nature.
This garden was never reached…
But on the steep paths of the world
in the midst of wars and famine
vines and roses multiply and entwine,
emissaries of happiness
and a more beautiful future.

In defence of didactic poetry

Warning to the reader:
what you are about to read
perhaps won't tally
with your idea of poetry
(and perhaps you're right,
perhaps it isn't
what should be called poetry).
These days it's widely held
that poets should watch out
not to say too much.
To write, is to allow
a mouth to speak from the shadows
and if poets have something to say
it can only be with closed eyes…
However, when beauty truth and justice
appeared to man as one thing
science couldn't do without poetry
and poets taught about the world's beauty.
If poets taught
it's because they have a lot to learn.
Because to teach and to learn are the same thing.
Only the person who won't learn refuses to teach.
Today, when we are much more knowledgeable
we are still ignorant of the formula
for living together on earth.
So we still have much to learn:
well then
let's not be afraid to teach.

Song of opposites

From night day is born,
and the warmth of summer
from the cold of winter.
And the water which falls from the sky
is born from drought below.
And life from death,
because the living is born from the inanimate.
And death from life itself.
One without the other doesn't work
but they contest with one another
and aren't themselves
except in this struggle which opposes and unites them.
In this way the balance of the world is established
And thus the ever out-of-balance world evolves.
Surmounting its contradictions,
living and proliferating,
improving itself all the while
such is the law of life
from which
(luckily for us)
we can't escape.

Eulogy and condemnation of work

Are you strong enough to sing of the inhuman work of men?
Man's achievements, his passing contradictions,
   the ever more complex construction of his honeycombed palaces
in his kingdom of the bees?
Have you the heart to sing of the heartless law of men
whose every new conquest is paid for
by a new mutilation?
Will you find the words to dispel the ancient curse?
For thousands of years we have advanced like a procession of
   dockhands, to erect new pyramids.
We raise into the sky cathedral arches where only
   our fantasies can live,
We build blind, black crystal towers,
Which admit into their heads buzzing with missiles
   nothing but the murderous swarm of figures
from the Stock Exchange and world trade.
We are capable of miracles in the midst of horror.
We do our best to make our home
   uninhabitable.
And yet
We are also carpenters,
our hands good and precise with the wood,
we've always known how to build,
and we know, once the white roof-frame on the school's done
how to tie a bouquet of wild roses.
Peasant, chemist, metal-worker, pilot or computer expert,
We know the measure and the secret weight of things,
we organise metamorphoses,
master the dancing curve of the universe.
We could make this earth a home.

The world of divided men

Born from the division of labour
the system feeds on the division of men
from one another
and the division they maintain, engender and multiply
within themselves.
So we live in the age of divided men
the age of division
of work and of richness
of production and exchange
of progress and modernity
of the heart and of reason
of the body and the mind
of science and the dream
of the useful and the beautiful
of art and life
of morality and politics
because the division of labour
which never stops perfecting itself as it moves
is the condition of efficiency
and the reason for absurdity.

The achievements of capitalism

So this system will have achieved miracles before our very eyes:
under its reign abundance reveals itself the cause of poverty,
progress engenders barbarism,
the strengthening of the State, insecurity,
the development of media
under-information,
the scintillating conquests of science
generalised ignorance,
economic globalisation
tribal wars,
the unification of the world market
the division of workers and peoples,
as for artists
all that remains for them
is to produce commodities
and to cultivate ugliness.

On the progressive character of war

Heavens! How war brings benefits to humanity
By the progress of science and technology.
In his time, thanks to his conquests, Alexander the Great
sent to his master Aristotle,
strange animals and the wonders of nature
he encountered.
And it's thanks to his war trophies
the first of his museums
was dedicated to the Muses in Alexandria.
Henceforth, we can't count
the advances we owe to war:
the invention of the catapult,
the battlements at Vauban,
the Zeppelin,
mustard gas,
the art of the statue
in the monuments to the dead of the Great War,
the atomic bomb,
star wars
and the possible destruction of humanity...
But the greatest progress all the wars we've fought could
bring us
would be peace and to say enough is enough.
War is natural amongst querulous people
but from that nature, it's time to break free
as the butterfly
from the prison of its chrysalis.

Navvies' song

(during a moment of tiredness, on a break)

It's true,
we've shifted mountains
but valleys too
and some dark precipices...
there's more than enough there to condemn us!
Yes, they've something on their plate those who demand
the closure of the great building site
and the throwing on the dole
of builders and navvies
Because we've
lifted mountains
and discovered precipices...
And many, among those who survive stuck
in the boxed-in valleys of mediocre life,
use it as a reason to keep their arms crossed.
All the same we must
have a go at mountains
drill tunnels
find new roads
squares and avenues.
all the same we must
dig the foundations
for the new houses where our children will live
and let their rooms be bigger and more airy
and let everyone have his right to his bit of light.

The modern Vulgate

O my human brothers have pity on us

Knowing the fate in store for us, my brothers
Often my heart shrinks, I'm very anxious for us
We walk the streets armed to the teeth
And yet as guileless as children
Trying to earn it we often lose our life
And living simply is often a torment

O my human brothers have pity on us

O my brothers sunk in the anonymous war
Gladiators in the arena assassins and victims
Cut price men, women, useless hands and hearts
Auctioned workers and the spring we destroy
My poor humanity divorced from itself
Running on its path without knowing where it leads

O my human brothers have pity on us

Strange is our accustomed world
Where abundance itself is the source of poverty
Where the more progress man makes the more he despairs
Where the greater his strength the greater his weakness
Where what he uses to conquer is what hurts him
Where he imprisons himself by escaping
Where his very freedoms are prisons
All our accomplished powers hold us to ransom
Because we aren't masters of our lives
We dominate the world and are dominated
By the hidden forces of our destiny
Whose name is sad and sordid self-interest

O my human brothers have pity on us
What's the use of praying to God and powerful men
When it's on ourselves our fate depends

O my human brothers have pity on us.

THE PRECURSORS' BOOK

The ages of humanity

According to Hesiod, humanity passed through several ages:
The Golden Age
when humans still lived
in the company of innocent
beautiful and happy gods;
The Silver Age, during which the decline began,
The Bronze Age, still primitive,
and finally the Iron Age
(the dark and violent time
in which he lived).
Since then,
historians
archaeologists
palaeontologists
have established a different order
according to which
humanity didn't fall but ascended.
Thus, everyone knows that after the stone age
came the bronze age
then the iron age
which preceded ours.
The question which should be asking now is:
When will we finally leave behind the age of brass?

The tall grasses

I EULOGY OF PRIMITIVE COMMUNITY
In the beginning was community
not the isolated individual, not the lord
    and the slave
but the human being, member of a community
the same as others and equal to others.
No-one dominated and no-one was dominated
and in the community of poverty all were rich
in community.
No-one could survive without others
And no-one made sense without others.
Man never went alone and naked across the plains.
Never was he a fallen god.
(Man in truth existed before existing).

He who walked in the tall grass
on the lookout, his assegai in his hand
possessed the beauty of the animals he hunted.
And the woman bent over the stream to drink
was its likeness, alive, fresh and transparent
pure and dark like the nocturnal entrails of the earth
because men and women who live at one
with their world live in beauty.
And men and women
Who don't know the shame of being domesticated
live in nobility
(which civilization has always recognised in primitive peoples.)
The universe itself had meaning
And those who didn't know the alphabet
could read its story in the wind in the branches
the stream's murmur, the tracks of animals.
Every movement had its reason,
every stone its history
the trees were great ancestors who watched over
    the village
the birds brought messages,
everything which lived and breathed

everything which was, alive or inanimate, had a soul.
In the beginning the earth wasn't fenced
and the wind circulated freely.
The seasons followed one another and men and women
lived according to their rhythm.
The world belonged to them.

II CRITIQUE OF PRIMITIVE COMMUNITY
The world belonged to them
but their world was limited to the light of a clearing
or the bed of a valley.
Beyond reigned the terror of the unknown.
Paradise was populated by ferocious animals.
Fear of night, thunder and spirits prevailed
and above all
the fear of other men.
In those distant times
the most gentle creatures devoured one another.
No-one had the right to exist without others
and the word freedom didn't yet exist.
Everyone obeyed the communal laws
the elders and the spirits.

The entire universe belonged to them
and they were the prey of the entire universe.

God didn't expel Adam and Eve from paradise.
They left
(it was too cold).
They left
to exchange animal skins
shells and fruit
to invade other territories
conquer the world
which was already theirs
and to become themselves.

The war of the gods

In the beginning was the epic.
The earth was populated by gods
and gods made war.
Marduk who had two pairs of eyes
Fought against his mother, Tiamat
and her eleven mercenaries,
the Viper, the Dragon, the Mammoth, the giant Lion,
the Mad Dog and the Scorpion Man, led by
        Kingu.
Baal, the king of the air and rain, against Mot, the god
         Of drought and Yamm, the god of the sea
And Mot against Astar,
The little god of irrigation honoured by farmers.
All fought for the control of the heavens
and the control of the earth.
Insufferable band
they spread among men
evils and benefits
catastrophes and victories
and made order and disorder, fear and civilisation
reign on earth.
Then, finally men
got the better of the first gods.
Today, no-one fears them any longer.
But the new gods,
in spite of their human appearance,
are much more terrifying.
They have much more sophisticated weapons,
Guns with infra-red sights,
spy satellites,
self-guiding bombs with auto-directing warheads,
laser beams for surgical strikes,
long-distance chemical weapons,
intercontinental nuclear missiles,
tanks armed with depleted uranium,
States and television channels,
courts, banks

international organisations,
good reasons and a good conscience...
The universe is nothing but an electronic game for them
where the enemy always rises up again and death
has no meaning.
The new gods unleash storms in
                the desert
and leave behind only charred bodies.
They fight for control of black gold,
and to impose their laws on others.
As under Hammourabi
men and women are condemned
to slavery for debt
they have a ring put through their nose
and they are sold in public squares.
The new gods bring the reign of disorder,
they corrupt the earth and hearts,
and set peoples at war with one another.
The new gods prepare star wars
the Apocalypse
which the ancients were content to dream about.
Let a new Flood sweep them away
greater than the Flood told about
twenty-five centuries before our era
in the eleventh tablet of the book of Gilgamesh!
And once more let life be saved
by the Arc of solidarity!

The revolt of the living-dead

For twenty years
thanks to a hundred thousand men
taking turns every three months
peasants from all over Egypt were mobilised
to build the pyramid of Cheops.
The Pharaohs' State
made necessary by the great works of irrigation
in the Nile Valley
now drained in its direction and for its exclusive profit,
by all the channels of power,
thanks to its priests, soldiers and scribes,
the river of men, of harvests of riches.
To guarantee eternal life to the living God
many men had to die.
The slaves of the High Empire
had given themselves the name
of the living-dead.
But neither the priests of Thebes,
nor the fear of Amon,
nor pikes nor blades
could guarantee to the power of the Pharaohs
of whatever epoch, eternal life.
In the eighteenth century before our epoch
the whole Empire was shaken by a great revolt
of peasants, artisans and slaves.
They seized the Palace
dethroned the Pharaoh, expelled the priests,
they exhumed the mummies from the tombs and the
pyramids,
they took hold of the storehouses of the palace and the
temples
they shared the food amongst themselves
and destroyed all the taxation documents.
According to legend, the earth began to run
widdershins
like a potter's wheel

because the insurgents moved into their masters' houses,
wore their clothes
and forced them to work on their behalf.
The people who with their hands gave form to life
showed they could destroy
even if they didn't yet know how to use their hands
to shape a new life
(that would go on a long time).
Then, the nomadic tribes of Hyksos
who dominated Egypt for a hundred and fifty years, spread out.
But, like Osiris who is forever reborn,
the seed buried in the night
springs to life from the soil in the light.

The Book of Isaiah

'They will build houses and live in them
They will plant vines and eat their fruit
They will no longer plant so that others might eat
Because the days of my people
Will be like the days of a tree
And my chosen ones will use what their hands have made.'
So Isaiah described the New Jerusalem
(because communism is an ancient need).
And because utopias are as old as him
He added: *'The lion will lie down with the lamb.'*
But in those days wolves hardly allowed themselves
to be moved by sermons.
That's the reason the prophet Isaiah
(in the year 690 BC)
died, by order of King Manasseh,
cut lengthways by a wood saw.

Orpheus's initiates

By the dance of the sun and sleep,
by Apollo and Dionysus,
by the vine which dies in winter to be reborn in spring,
they were initiated, they knew the songs,
the great circle of the universe and the secret of life
through which everything which lives dies and is reborn
and that of purification of the spirit which always renews itself.
From the Mysteries of Eleusis, away from the fear
and the customs of official religion,
they devoted a cult to universal life.
Helios, who is called Dionysus,
he alone is Orcus, he alone is Zeus
and Zeus contains everything,
the whole body of Zeus contains the brilliant heights of
    the vast ether
the hugeness of the sea and the glorious earth.
It's he who governs the winds and the currents of the sea,
it's he who holds the power of fire and makes mountains tremble.
But it's said too that the second Dionysus
was torn to shreds by the Titans
for having wanted to steal the secrets of the infernal Forges
and that Zeus ate his heart.
Then he came to life in Dionysus Iacchos, he who exults,
he who preserves the joy of the wheel of the transient.
They were the first to be conjured up by beauty and happiness.
They opened the way for philosophers
poets and utopians.

Such was the first amongst them, Orpheus
who returned from the kingdom of the dead,
son of the forests who calmed wild beasts
and healed men with his song.

(In the beginning was the word
– that too was an augury –
because man is born in man's song).

Empedocles' sandals

The summer winds from the Aeolian coasts
rush over the gulf of Sicily.
They shake the tresses of the olive trees and the myrtles
and raise white waves on the Ionian sea.
One day when the north wind was so strong
it snatched the fruit from the trees
they say Empedocles burnt donkeys
and stretched their hides on the hilltops
to stop it blowing.
The sun, high in the sky above the violet waters
of deep Charybdis, is like a chariot wheel
at its zenith.
The sea is the earth's froth...
On days of celebration, the citizens of Agrigente
have processions on horseback
carrying burning torches in their hands.
Light runs like water down the hills
into the streets and the harbour.
Empedocles the wise, the scholar and magus,
is amongst them
upright on a chariot driven by the Muses,
dressed in gold and purple,
he wears on his head a Delphic crown
and on his feet bronze sandals.
The world is one, says the poet.
It hasn't come into being.
For all eternity it has been made up of its four elements:
Zeus lighting fire, Hera bringing life to the earth,
Adonis to the air and Nestis to the water.
Forever changing, it never stops...
The universe is a sphere divided in two
in its upper part reigns fire
in its lower dark
which by their rotation produce day and night.
Sometimes love unites everything
Sometimes hate splits in two,
Eros and Polemos share the world between them
In an endless combat.

The universal attraction of desire
and the repulsion of centrifugal forces
thus move everything...
But by his death above all Empedocles
        guaranteed his immortality.
One morning, he would have climbed the slopes of the volcano
And would have thrown himself in Etna's crater.
Near a bush, his disciples, set out in search,
find one of his sandals
Since that day the mystery remains unsolved.
Did he want to melt into the great whole
to finally discover the secret of the universe?
By disappearing did he want to live eternally leaving
in this sandal a proof of his disappearance?
Unless it was a set up
to escape his persecutors.
They say, in fact
that being wholeheartedly for democracy
Pythagoras's disciple
had to go into exile in the Peloponnese
where he ended his days.

Heraclitus' river

'We bathe
And we can't bathe in the same river twice.'
Asserted Heraclitus of Ephesus, the so-called obscure,
Who clearly understood the law of becoming.
'That which is contrary is useful
And it's from things in struggle
That harmony is born.
Everything is made from discord...'
But what's happened to our river?
Sometimes it hangs around lazy and despairing
and soaks into the sands
sometimes it gets carried away and leaves its bed,
sometimes it alters its course
and reshapes the look of the land.
If it knows its source it's always unaware
of where its mouth will be and where it will end up
and ever renewing itself
it remains always the same.

Thinking about Democritus

About Democritus we know little
he travelled and was ruined
he was, so they say, somewhat conservative and misogynistic
and laughed at anything.
(But those things hardly make him interesting…)

Before Democritus the sea was full of monsters
and the air, of gods;
every worldly mystery
had a simple and miraculous explanation.
The tears of Dionysus's sisters
punished by the Gods for having tried to save their brother
fell into the waves and turned into amber
(from which we get the word electricity).
And there was no need to understand
as magic was in everything.

But Democritus wanted to understand
and armed with nothing more than intuition, reason and
       poetry
he dreamed of science and anticipated it.

At the origin of things, he said, are atoms and emptiness
and atoms in movement
are caught in a vortex and accumulate.
They are infinite and indivisible.
Nothing is born from nothingness nor returns to nothingness.
Worlds are without limit, they breed and perish.
Stars are rocks
and the earth is a hollow disk
which floats on the air thanks to its lightness.
In the beginning, it wandered here and there due to its smallness
then, in time, it grew denser and became weighty.
The soul too is made of atoms, smooth and round
it's the lightest body, the most perfect, the igneous body
but the soul is perishable and dies with the flesh.

Epicurus, who came afterwards,
also thought the world was formed of atoms
and that everything had weight,
everything obeyed the universal law of gradients.
It's because atoms follow a descending curve
that they can meet and create matter.
Everything is attraction and repulsion.
The foundation of the universe is atoms
and their solidity.
Everything is union and contradiction.

In this world
from which they began to expel gods
the individual
– an atom lost in its orbit
can in this way overcome the pain of being alone
knowing he is an atom in the universe.
But still today,
in the sidereal world of technology and capitalism
where power, knowledge and emptiness rule,
individuals, free and solitary electrons,
revolve yet in the darkness
in search of the nucleus
of love
and unity.

Socrates and Xanthippe

Xanthippe, woman of the people and wife of Socrates,
was in the habit, so they say, when he came home
to have a drink with his friends
of insulting her philosopher husband.
Sometimes should would kick him out and throw rubbish over him
treating him as a waster.
(And no doubt, she had her reasons…)
One day, Antisthenes,
– himself well know for his bad ways –
asked Socrates why he kept such a shrew.
To which the philosopher is reputed to have replied:
'To become a good rider
you choose a difficult horse.
That's why I, who want to get on with everyone,
chose her,
convinced that if I could put up with her,
I could easily get along with anybody.'
(From this marital tale
maybe we can draw a few ideas
about politics and democracy).

Socrates and the banquets

In *The Republic,* Plato grants to Socrates
the idea of setting up a class of warriors
responsible for watching over the City.
They would live together
sharing their property
and that of their wives and children.
In this way he intended to assure the unity of the City.
Also, regularly,
like the Lacedaemonians
they would eat together.
(From ancient communism,
it's surely this last custom
which today
has the most supporters).

The death of Socrates

On the eve of his death
(when all Athens
was waiting at the port
for the return of the sacred vessel
loaded with presents for Apollo's temple)
Socrates
– condemned for having
through his teaching
corrupted the youth of the City –
got himself ready
(to spare the women
the task)
then he asked for a lute so he could learn to play.
People were astonished: why such a wish
and at such a moment
from a man
who had never touched the instrument?
– Simply, replied Socrates
for the pleasure of learning to play the lute.

Discussion on the communists of antiquity

– They criticised private property
  as the root of iniquity and jealousy.
– That hasn't changed much.
– According to them, the world was made by the gods,
  it didn't belong to men.
– Man as the master and owner of nature,
  we see where that has led us...
– They preached collective ownership
– Others, in every age have done the same
– And also women held in common.
– For them, were women property?
– So, they said no woman will belong to a single man
  and no man to a single woman.
– We would have to decree
  a community of men and women...
– They advocated a frugal life
  but above all appreciated happiness.
– On this point, we can agree.
– Their democracy was reserved for aristocrats and their
  communism for an initiated elite, warriors and poets.
– This shocks us most, but we need to reflect on it too...
– In truth they were nostalgic for a golden age,
  for what existed before
  the division of labour and commercial relationships.
– We too, we dream of a golden age;
  but we situate it in the future.
– Their golden age was nothing
  but the elaborated memory of primitive communism.
  At that time, progress took place through the dissolution
  of the existing community.
– Today technological progress
  still takes place most often
  through the destruction of human relations.
– Their communism was reactionary.
– Can ideas about the future ignore the dreams of the past?

Two lessons from Alexander

I
Alexander the Great made himself famous
by a sword-stroke
in the Temple of Zeus
in the former capital of the kings of Phrygia
by which he cut the knot
no-one could untie
and opened the route to Asia Minor.
(Sometimes it's by drastic measures
we resolve the thorniest questions
because there's a time for reflection
and a time for action).

II
Once he'd conquered half the world
he asked himself what he could do with it.
How could he maintain this great vanquished empire
Which would soon disintegrate?
He couldn't even manage to hang onto his soldiers.
Once arrived in the Indus Valley
they were fed up and took it into their heads
to give up and go home.
(There's a time for action
and a time for reflection)

Spartacus

The sun at its zenith above the ring is pitiless.
Nothing can be expected from it,
it lays men low, saps energy
and wipes out all spirit of resistance.
All the same, Spartacus is training in the arena,
the ex-Thracian shepherd, child of Orpheus's country
sold as a slave for having deserted from the Roman army.
Spartacus doesn't want to end up like an animal
deprived of freedom.
In the evening, near the stalls,
he talks quietly to the other gladiators.
And those who'll have to fight each other
to the death in the arena
protected and hidden by their breast-plates and their helmets
outside the arena let down their guard
find they're brothers and
to make a life from now on
they'll have to fight not one another
but together.
Sick to death
of killing one another
for the pleasure of their masters
they're dying to give them their chance to die.
Their plot let out of the bag, with sixty-three companions,
Spartacus flees the gladiator school and leaves
        Capua.
Then they arrive at Vesuvius where they set up camp
        in the middle of the vines.
Soon, the slaves from the great southern estates,
shepherds from the Apennines,
prisoners from the Germanic wars
Greeks, Orientals, Frenchmen,
also free men
came and join them
and the sixty-three were soon sixty thousand then
        a hundred.
And the sun at its zenith in the sky
couldn't stop them.

Everywhere they went
they pillaged, killed the owners
and made everything common.
They forced a way through to the Alps,
took apart the two Roman legions of
Varinius Glaber and Publius Valerius,
held out for three years
and made Rome tremble.
They'd taken up the flame of the first rebels.
Those who had neither a poet to sing their glory
nor a philosopher in their ranks
did what was never done in the communism of the philosophers:
threatened the slave-owners' power.
The Senate in a panic sent an army of six legions against them
led by Crassus.
The rebels wanted to get to Sicily
but the gods weren't with them
the storm broke their rafts
and it was near the Apulian coast
they had to stand and fight.
They brought Spartacus a horse,
he killed it with his sword and said:
'A victor I'll be able to choose the best,
vanquished I won't need one.'
And there he fought amongst his own kind
and amongst his own kind he was killed.
Afterwards, Crassus,
all the way from Rome to Capua,
to dispel the fear of the owners
and to strike fear into the dispossessed,
had six thousand rebellious slaves crucified
who died beneath the setting sun
having lived in the free morning air.

On a theme from Horace

(after the Epistle to Julius Florus)

To a correspondent, Horace tells the story
of one of Lucullus's soldiers
(Lucullus, the victor over Mithridates
known for his wealth, his fasts and his banquets).
This soldier
– no doubt a poor peasant from Latium –
had saved, with great difficulty, a little nest-egg
which he kept, tucked in his belt.
One night, while he was sleeping, dog-tired, in the camp,
snoring away, someone stole his belt.
When he woke up, he was like a rabid wolf,
livid, he had it in for the whole earth
including himself...
and when he had to go and fight,
single-handedly he ousted Mithridates' guard
from a heavily fortified position.
His general congratulated him, gave him a medal
and twenty thousand sesterces
But soon, they had to launch a new attack.
So the general called him and said:
'Go where your courage calls you!
Your reward won't be less than you deserve.'
Our hero
Whose courage no doubt summoned him home
replied:
'Send instead a soldier who's lost his belt.'
(Thus, even back then,
the rich sent the poor to fight for them
and they fought all the better
if they were robbed of hope.
All the same some, even then, jibbed...)

On the greatness and decadence of Antiquity

So, we must recognise
that nothing which has provoked centuries of admiration –
the pyramids of Egypt and the Valley of Kings,
the grandeur of the Parthenon and the Coliseum,
the Colossus of Rhodes and democracy,
or even the ancient ideal of beauty and harmony,
no, nothing of all that would have been possible
without the millions of slaves who could be worked to death
or thrown to the muraenas.
But slaves have a fault:
you can't count on them.
In spite of the severe edicts of Octavius
(for every proprietor killed
all the slaves of the household must die)
they rebelled fairly often.
They were also generally lazy.
Further, their patriotism had limits…
As early as the Peloponnesian wars
those from Athens had made an alliance with Sparta.
And when the troops of the barbarian Alaric
were on the ramparts of Rome
it was the slaves who opened the doors to them.
So those who made the greatness of Rome
also brought about its fall.

Mo-Zi

In ancient China there was a philosopher of the poor.
He was called Mo-Zi, came from the working class
and bore a name which indicated the ignominy of slavery.
Mo-Zi went from village to village
and he preached to the people in the poor areas.
He taught them not to respect the hierarchy
and the rites of Confucianism,
to respect only what's useful
and to disdain warmongers
because 'the most glorious conqueror
is a murderer beyond compare,
a greater criminal than any assassin…'
He preached the doctrine of universal love,
an egalitarian and frugal communism
founded on common ownership
and the participation of everyone in productive work.
After having tried in vain to dissuade the warrior princes,
and as he had many enemies,
he, the pacifist, decided to take up arms to defend peace
and organised a feared military sect.
He was a practical philosopher
and an effective propagandist.
One day, someone reproached him:
Why did he put himself out to pursue men?
Shouldn't the wise man stay at home
like the pretty girl
waiting for suitors?
To which he replied:
– We live in troubled times.
Lots of people will run after a pretty girl.
But not many seek out a good man.
You have to use violence too so people will listen.

The Xian army

In Xian there lived an emperor
who, dreaming of eternal glory,
had twelve thousand clay infantrymen made
to immortalise his army.
But the glory of armies is fragile,
and, contemplating his troops today
it's the work of the potters we admire.

Lao Zi's luggage

I
We don't know much about old Lao Zi,
he had a lump on his forehead
and was fond of playing the fool
(because the wise man conceals his wisdom).

II
Hidden away in the mountains, he disdained honours,
wealth, power and study.
(He'd left Tcheou's house
before it was replaced by the T'sin.)

III
'Imagine that the world is ravine,' he would say,
'If the rivers and seas rule over the valleys
it's because they set themselves lower.'
He taught the power of frailty.

IV
'Whoever claims to lead the people must be its follower.'
By preaching wou-wei, the art of non action, he acted
and everyone could find their way by following his.
In this way, Tao was wisdom and magic, resignation and
    Revolt.

V
When he went north, the guardian of the pass
as payment for his passage, made him recite the Tao-To-King
(because the Tao was his only luggage).
In this way, he reached the land of the Immortals.

Remembering the sermon on the mount

'Blessed are the poor for theirs is the Kingdom of God'.
Speaking to the crowd gathered on the hill, Jesus took sides.
God goes barefoot, he lines up with the oppressed.
'It will be more difficult,' he said 'for a rich man
              to enter the Kingdom of God
than for a camel to pass through the eye of a needle.'
In his eyes, the Kingdom of God was not exclusively about the
    after-life;
he declared its triumph on earth
in community, love and equality.
It's said of the Apostles they held everything in common
and enjoyed great grace.
Jesus believed in the power of love.
'Love your enemies, do good to those who hate you,'
he said, 'pray for those who persecute you.'
People didn't always understand.
(But do class consciousness and hatred of injustice
exclude love of humanity?
And mustn't oppressors be set free too?)
Jesus advocated non-violence.
All the same it's said he went into the Temple
Overturned the tables of the money-changers, the seats of
    the pigeon-sellers
and expelled the merchants from the house of God
because he knew the worth of anger.
It's true he also said:
'If someone hits you, turn the other cheek,
you will be a son of the Almighty.'
And himself he went willingly to the cross....
(But for a long time
martyrdom – either by self-immolation or hunger strike –
will remain a form of struggle
and among the most effective
because the blood of martyrs sows the seeds of dawn.)
To his followers he announced one day:
'Everyone will hate you because of my name...'
because he knew what revolutionaries and
everyone who stands up to authority have to put up with.

But as far as the pitfalls of power go
(which await even revolutionaries)
he gave his friends a warning:
'Whoever amongst you wants to be great
let him be your servant...'
and also: 'The Son of Man came
not to be obeyed
but to obey.'
In truth,
To change the world,
Jesus believed in the power of the word and example.
And he didn't change the world
And yet he changed it.

The parable of Jesus and Caesar

When Jesus was in the Temple
some Pharisees and followers of Herod wanted to
    confuse him.
They asked him questions designed to trap him
so they could hand him over to the authorities.
– We see that you talk straight and teach truth,
Should we pay the tribute to Caesar?
Jesus who could think on his feet replied:
– Why are you putting me to the test?
Bring me a coin, let me see it.
Then, the coin in his hand, he asked:
Whose image is this and whose inscription?
– Caesar's, they answered.
– Then give to Caesar what is Caesar's
And to God what is God's…
In this way perhaps he wanted to keep his message
safe for a while from Roman power.
(You can't fight on all fronts at once.)
Perhaps too he who was known as the king of the Jews
wanted to protect himself from the temptations of power
and from his own weaknesses.
So the word of Christ
which wanted to live beyond the power of Rome
made its appearance there.
While the poor, slaves, the lower classes came to him
and they lived in secret communities
hiding in the catacombs, drawing fish and birds on walls,
teaching disdain of the powerful, the power of love,
equality and eternal life,
his disciples were persecuted, thrown to the lions and massacred
and their resignation was admired by everyone.
So the rich too came to church
the powerful looked on it differently,
named deacons and bishops
and finally Constantine established Christianity as the
    official Roman religion.
But by conquering the Rome of the Caesars
of course God lost his soul.

The purveyor of miracles

Jesus is credited with numerous miracles
(in ancient stories, people gave credit to the poor).
So, he walked on water
(even then, you needed to do a lot
to attract attention
and impress crowds)
changed water into wine and made loaves multiply
(which is definitely what we're still after).
He made the lame whole
(because he came as a doctor
not as a conqueror)
opened hearts,
restored the hearing to the deaf
and made the mute speak
(which tells us he was a teacher
and a propagandist without equal).
And, to end beautifully,
three days after being crucified
he came back from the dead.
(But that, after all, is what usually happens
to great hopes).

San Francesco, il Poverello

During a time of great chaos, violence,
        dishonesty,
heresy and revolt
young Giaccomo leaves his family and friends
        from the gilded youth of Assisi;
he gives up parties, games, his troubadour tricks
        and his dreams of knighthood
to devote himself to the service of god.
'Go, Francois, repair my crumbling house,' his Lord said to him.
So with his bare hands he begins to rebuild churches,
then, as the curious and disciples come running
he founds a community of the poor
which soon grows and becomes the Infant Brothers order.
Meeting a leper as he leaves Assisi
he kisses his hand
because, for him, Christ is love, poverty and joy.
Often afterwards he'll share his coat
refusing for himself and his brothers any wealth
any possession.
'Go and preach… Have in your purse
no gold, no silver, no coins, no scrip for the journey…'
Jesus had said.
So, with his brothers, he sets off on the dusty roads
of his native Umbria,
in the heavy white light, on the roads of Italy,
in Tuscany or in the France he loves and where he got his
        name,
to preach universal and angelic love.
Lord be praised, and all your creatures
in particular Brother Superior the Sun
he sings in his canticles.
Lord be praised for all the creatures living on
        earth
even the earthworms he carefully collects
because Jesus once compared himself to them.
Sometimes he stops in an olive grove or
        a scrubby field

and raising his arms to the sky
he lets forth a prayer to the birds
inviting them to sing their thanks to their Creator
and the birds do sing…
In the same way
he goes into the towns and preaches harmony and charity
to the merchants.
He calls on the rich to give their wealth to the poor,
and some do give, (at least a little).
For him, love and harmony must be a personal
    creed,
but also the creed of the community and of the world.
He extols class reconciliation
and they say he even converted that wolf Gubbio…
He orders his brothers to live frugally
to possess nothing, to work on farms or in towns
and if they don't earn enough, to beg.
(Later, his disciples will often fall out
because there'll always be some who in the eyes of others
don't stick close enough to the rules).
Everywhere, Francesco, the little bearded man
whose enthusiasm is catching,
sings the glory of Christ.
He gives the example of the renunciation of earthly goods.
He remains the shining image of the spirit of innocence and
    joy.
But if the one they christened il Poverello
loved the poor so
he never encouraged them to fight against poverty.
He loved them because they were made in Christ's image,
he loved them because he loved their poverty.
(In the centuries which followed
many who fought the arrogance of wealth
in search of salvation went astray in the same way).

The Qarmatians' revolt

for Tahar Ouettar

*Who then will rediscover the traces of the Qarmatians
and who will follow in their footsteps?*

Their name is lost in the desert sand
carried away by the wind, scattered among stones.
All the same, their reign lasted a hundred years
in southern Iraq, in Syria, in the gulf of Bahrain...
Ishmaelite Muslims undaunted and sacrilegious
they neither prayed nor fasted
and had no mosques.
(It's also said of them they held women
    in common).
They left behind a reputation as pillagers
who attacked caravans and pilgrims.
For a century they threatened the caliph of Baghdad
and the princes of Damascus.
In defiance, they stole the black stone of Mecca
and kept it seven years
before returning it, broken in seven pieces.

Who will rediscover the traces of the Qarmatians?

Legend has it they established a republic;
They elected a council of six wise men who spoke
    with modesty and moderation;
they sent missionaries into the towns and villages
to convince the inhabitants to practise ulfa, the
    common ownership of goods.
They assembled cattle, sheep, jewels,
    food
and everyone brought what they had:
the women, what they earned from weaving
the children, the birds they hunted in the fields...
No-one owned anything
(apart from his sword and his weapons).

Who will rediscover the traces of the Qarmatians
And who will follow in their footsteps?

Amongst them the land belonged to the community
so no-one needed to own private wealth
    as the entire earth belonged to everyone.
The houses of the poor and sick were repaired
    by everyone.
They clothed the naked and saw to their
    needs.
The corn was ground without charge in public mills,
Commercial transactions were carried out through non
transferable
    tokens
and the State took care that no member of the community
suffered hunger or poverty.
There were neither taxes nor tithes
(but thirty thousand black slaves served the community).

So who will rediscover the traces of the Qarmatians?
When one of their number, Sahib al Shama, the man
    with the black she-camel, was taken prisoner,
the caliph ordered all his limbs to be amputated,
before having his head cut off and displaying the bits of his
    body
on the squares and bridges of Baghdad
to edify and terrify the people.
In this way the Qarmatians' example was wiped out
like the traces of the executed prisoner's dried blood
scattered in the dust across the town.

But on the edge of the desert
    from time to time,
            there reappears like a mirage
rising with the sand,
    the silhouette of the rebels,
        horsemen of the wind and the clouds.

A tomb for the peasants

When he who from dawn to dusk every day
            bends to the earth
lifts his eyes to the sky
and sees the injustices committed in his name
he demands a settling of accounts.

Why must the vassal who feeds monks and knights
die of hunger?

The lords who are supposed to look after the peasants
pass through the fields, pillage the harvests
and put the country at their mercy.

They impose drudgery, they take the lion's share
            for themselves and don't carry out their duty.

In the woodlands, in a field close to an oak copse
            the peasants have gathered.

Here they are, lord, establishing a parliament
            and forming a commune
– hence the long-standing insult of the term –

Here the beasts of burden, instead of keeping as they should
            their brows bowed to the earth, dare to raise their eyes.

They take hold of their scythes, their sticks
            their pikes
and head for the castles.
But ill befalls those who ask justice of the powerful.

Once the first fears have passed
the lords and their men-at-arms
are going to go hunting peasants like they go hunting hounds.

They're going to track them through the thickets, encircle
        them in the fields, drive them out of hiding
and massacre them.

They'll plunge them in molten lead or boiling pitch

they'll cook them slowly over small fires.

All the captured will have their hamstrings cut.

They'll cut off their ears, tear out their tongues or
        their eyes
so that those pardoned, out of Christian charity
will go into the countryside and wandering in the lanes
will teach others the terror of uprising.

As for the one who claimed to be the king of the peasants,
before,
        quartering him, they'll put a white hot iron crown
on his head.
And that is how things were done in the gentle country of
France
In the time of troubadours and courtly love, in the
        northern regions, close to the Norman lands
and the grass that grows sweetly in the breeze
        grows on their bones

and the earth that sleeps, like a pregnant woman,
        fecund in every springtime

is soaked in their blood.

The trial of Campanella

In his time Campanella had built, layer by layer on the clouds of
    a dream
a City of the Sun where all life would be submitted
to precise rules, where everything would be planned
like the movement of the burning stars around their frozen orbs
and it would fall to the priests (called 'Suns'
or 'Metaphysicians') to command everything
(including relations between the sexes).
Copulation itself would be governed by a magistrate
named Love, who, helped by matrons, would have to choose
partners, the time and perhaps also the most favourable position
for the propagation of the race.
Because every revolution, even that of the flesh
in its familiar orbit,
belongs to the great movement of the universe.
In 1599, the priest Campanella tried to raise the people
against the domination of Calabria by the Spaniards.
The Inquisition arrested him and tortured him seven times.
Finally, he sought refuge in France in the Jacobin convent
taking with him, like the sun of Greek fire, his scientific and
eugenic dream full of telescopes,
flying machines, and a life,
founded on the community of goods and women,
as regular as a solar system.
But the sun itself – all astrophysicists
    confirm –
is a very troublesome playmate
whose pranks are unpredictable.

Account of Thomas More's earthly journey

I
Thomas More lived on an island which wasn't called
      Utopia
it was one of the strangest places where wealth in common
      had been destroyed.
The fine arable lands no longer served the common
      good.
The nobles 'as lazy as drones' and hungry for luxury
      and money
drove the peasants from their lands,
stealing the clothes from their backs,
so they could use them to graze the flocks needed for the
      cloth industry.
At the time of the enclosures people said sheep
      ate people
and the peasants kicked out of the countryside were reduced
      to begging in the towns
where they were arrested, tortured and often hung
      because vagabondage was forbidden.
Lawyer for City merchants and the haberdashers'
      Corporation
he defended their interest against Dutch
      weavers
but he saw the damage done by private interests
from the very start of manufacturing.

II
Realist thinker, astute adviser, lawyer accustomed to settling
      practical questions,
he wrote Utopia because the most fundamental problems
of his society
couldn't be solved under the system of property.
Many of the ideas of his book were put into practice
Under capitalism… For example, colonies whose usefulness
      he'd imagined.
But also in the countries of actual and scientific socialism

(which all the same set no store by the dreams of the
          utopians).
Such it was, for example, in the case of sending young people
          to the countryside,
to perfect their education and help in the fields,
or the general austerity of habits and forced labour for
          the anti-social.
(A very liberal idea in a country where theft and
          vagabondage were punished by death.)
But many of his suggestions
(and some of the most beautiful) are still
          to be realised.

III

He was friends with Erasmus, the author of In Praise of Madness,
the two of them linked by a happy taste for the virtues of
          Reason.
Which didn't prevent him doing mad things;
because in an irrational State to claim to defend Reason
while serving the State is not rational.
Thomas More had good reason to distrust power,
he thought the wise man should remain at a distance from public
    affairs
all the same, he agreed to be part of the king's Council and became
          lord chancellor.
Great in heart and mind he was quickly
          promoted
and for the same qualities fell even more quickly.
A tolerant man, he couldn't support the king in
          his divorce.
And Henry VIII, (the humanists' hope) wouldn't tolerate him.
He who'd written that the Utopians possessed nothing
not even their houses (changed every ten years
          by lottery),
was expelled from his sweet Chelsea home, where he lived
in a studious and Christian harmony with his family,
on the orders
          of the king.
He who had always shown indifference
to money and rewards

and jewels for children's rattles
saw his fortune confiscated.
Then, as he was life's advocate,
he had his own taken from him.
The king condemned him to hanging
but, in a magnanimous gesture,
agreed he could be beheaded.
'God keep my friends from such a favour,'
said Thomas More who right to the end
revealed the happy nature and the humour
the king so liked.
As the scaffold was jerry built and wobbled
he said to the Tower guard:
'See me up safe,
 For my coming down, let me shift myself.'
Then, for the executioner, he added:
'Pick up thy Spirits, Man, and be not afraid
to do thine Office; my Neck is very short,
take heed therefore thou strike not awry
for having thine Honesty.'
So came to a premature end
Thomas More's stay
on a too solid planet.
But still today
all over the world
those who seek Utopia
replicate his journey.

The Maya's revolution

The sun is doing its rounds above the trees.
In the forest rises the city of pyramids.
Using their elbows, their knees, the players
make the ball fly, dancing in the dust
to stop it hitting the ground.
In the sky, the movement mustn't stop
and the ball flies through the stone ring
fixed to the temple wall.
The corn children honour the moon and the sun
they know the rotation of the planets
and can predict eclipses,
they command the circle
but they haven't invented the wheel...
(It takes time for people
to develop practical skills).
In the Palace, the young prince
Pierces his foreskin with a thorn.
To appease the gods he makes a gift
of a bit of his royal blood to his enslaved people.
(Something few of our politicians
would consent to).
The ball flies and the sun dances
on the field the rite must be carried through
the winner – supreme honour – will be sacrificed
so the sun will rise again.
(Let's imagine world champions
immolated live on screens around the world
as the entire planet applauds...)
But the glorious age of the beautiful game is past!
And it seems amongst the Maya themselves,
their ways having taken a turn for the worse, finally
it's the losers who are sacrificed.
(So, all religions
which start by pushing believers towards sacrifice
end by sacrificing unbelievers).
According to the law of universal rotation
everything passes over the horizon and all stars die.

One day the corn children had had enough of sacrificing themselves
for priests, warriors and kings.
They left the arrogant cities
and went back to live in the forests.

They are still there today.
And it happens in a village in Chiapas
Under the watch of Zapatista rifles,
ready to sacrifice so that life may flourish,
the children of the corn people play ball
while in the sky the sun does its rounds.

The war of the flowers

Listen to the song of the bird
Listen to the song of the bird with feathers of fire
He opens his wings in the sun
The Quetzal with purple feathers takes flight into the sun
He is the singer, he makes hearts light.

They go half naked across the plains, the children of the desert.
They have left the ancient city of Aztlan.
They are the Chichimecs of the Dog ancestry.
In front walk the priests carrying on their shoulders
The effigy of Huitzilopochtli, the humming bird of the left.

Listen to the song of the bird
Listen to the song of the bird of the children of the sun.

When they saw, standing on a cactus,
the eagle with a snake in its mouth
they knew they'd arrived and they stopped to establish
        their city
but soon the young prince married the daughter of the
    neighbouring king
and had her burnt as a sacrifice to the gods
and once more they were sent packing to the land of lakes near
        the rising sun
and they took refuge amongst the reeds
to cultivate tomatoes, breed turkeys
and carry out the sacrifices demanded by the gods.

Listen to the song of the birds
Listen to the song of the Lord of the Turquoises.

When the sun at the birth of the world almost died
the gods poured out their blood so it would be reborn.
Now, it's for men to sacrifice themselves
so the river of precious water will sing forever
of blood and day always follow night
above the emerald forests
where the birds with feathers of fire sing.

Listen to the song of the bird
Listen to the song of Quetzal with the spreading wings
Like a flower's bloom in the rising sun

The ancient Chichimecs became the Aztecs
the sun people.
They built the glorious city of Tenochtitlan
even more glorious than the legendary Tula of the Toltecs
and the most powerful empire under the sun.
Their merchants who criss-crossed the country were their
        spies.
They knew how to set tribes against one another
and impose their rules on all.
Only the priests didn't pay taxes.
They sent their warriors across the country
To wage 'the flower war'
and find prisoners to sacrifice.
They were the first Romans of America.
With each new conquest they adopted the gods
of the vanquished.

Listen to the song of the Bird
with feathers of fire
He is the Singer, he lightens hearts.

But as the Aztecs had vanquished
They were to be vanquished.
And the basis of their power became their weakness.
They who could have become a modern State
divided into classes and going out to conquer the world
were defeated the day they met their future.
When Montezuma saw in a dream warriors
with stags' feet and covered in armour
he thought Quetzalcoatl,
the ancient god stolen from the Toltecs had returned
and he knew the sun was about to set on Mexico.

But he didn't know the coming gods
were going to be much more bloodthirsty
than the ancient divinities.

Listen to the song of the Bird
Listen to the song of the flower people
Now the blood-stained gods are dying
That the reign of Xochipilli
The flower-god of joy, of love and fecundity
Who bedecks himself in pheasant feathers
Is arriving,
Now the reign of the true Quetzalcoatl
The plumed serpent
The master of earth and water
The inventor of art and technology
Quetzalcoatl the peaceable
Is upon us.

The end of the cannibals

When the Caribs
who populated the islands before the arrival of the Whites
invaded an Arawak village
they killed the men and ate them,
seized the women
kept the children
to castrate and fatten them
so they could be eaten later.
All we've retained of these people
– who we exterminated without eating –
is the word cannibal.
When the Whites arrived
Inspired by Christian faith and reason
they put an end to these despicable ways
by making the Arawaks and Caribs die of
        hunger;
they brought light by burning their homes;
they saved them from hell by shutting them underground
        in mines;
cured them of their taste for sodomy
by having them eaten by dogs;
finally, the accomplished a great step forward
for humanity in these islands
by establishing slavery.

The Haudenosaunee

Tired of the unending wars between the Iroquois,
the Mohawks and the other hill and plain peoples
the Peacemaker set up the Iroquois Confederation
– the Haudenosaunee –
the people who build the long house
a communal house 500 kilometres long
which brought together Oneidas, Senecas, Onandagas, Tuscaroras
Mohawks and Cayugas
And put an end to the wars between the Iroquois nations.
The men with the protuberant ears
impressed Franklin by their democratic
        organisation.
They lived in peace in towns protected by log fences,
Raised cattle, grew corn and fruit trees.
And men and women elected as equals a great council
where the chiefs came together on the order of their
        tribes.

But Iroquois democracy
Like all democracy – was also a State;
that is, a menace to other peoples
and in the end for its own people.
And the Peacemaker was also a conqueror.
At the time of the pelt wars
to ensure the monopoly of trade with the Whites
of the Atlantic
the Iroquois lay in wait along the rivers
burned the canoes, massacred the Indians
who traded with the French
and took hostages to negotiate with.
Armed by the English and the Dutch
they multiplied the raids against the Algonquins
and the Abenakis, destroyed their harvests
led their wives and children into captivity
and tortured their warriors to death.
They exterminated the Hurons.
In this way they carried out the work of the conquerors
who would become their masters
and destroy them.

The lost tribe

When the Europeans discovered America
the Indians discovered trade.
They who previously had lived solely
from hunting, fishing and agriculture
learned to hunt for otter, elk and beaver
so their skins could be sold to the white merchants.
'The beaver, so the saying goes, is versatile:
cauldrons, knives, mirrors, bradawls.'
And as the whites are numerous
and need lots of skins
because they live in an icy misty place
where it's best to stay wrapped warm
they had to give up fishing and growing
to devote themselves to skins
skins ever greater in number
to be stripped off and prepared
and which yielded less and less.
A Seminole tribe
Living on the Florida coast
realising they were being robbed
one day decided to do without middlemen.
So all of them
men, women and children,
piled their produce in long canoes
and set off at high tide for the White Man's country
which must be hidden, there,
just over the horizon.
No-one came back.
Victims, among others, of the discovery of capitalism.

THE BOOK OF REVOLUTIONARY DAYS

Is he good, is he bad?

Diderot is sitting, in his dressing gown, at his desk.
He stops writing for a moment
and rests the quill against his lips.
'Is he good, is he bad?'
Perhaps he's thinking of his philosopher friends
Who are obsessed with this question too.
Rousseau the best of men
The author of Emile, this great sensitive heart,
to whom one would grant absolution without confession
and who put his five children into care.
Or Voltaire, that devil of a man,
the refugee from the chateau of Ferney
This man of sarcasm, this cynic, this misanthrope
Who becomes enraged when a certain Calas
Whom he doesn't even know, suffers an injustice.
'Is he good, is he bad?'
His play is causing him trouble
It's the title which will please him most
The question deserved to be asked.
(Since the gas chambers at least
We know he's capable
Of the worst as of the best).
'Is he good is he bad?'
Each time they tried to dismiss it
The question came back through the window
Like this fly which comes through the casement
And makes the philosopher raise his head.
What is he thinking about at this moment?
Perhaps the chambermaid
Ah! human nature…
'Is he good, is he bad?'
Man is not what he is,
He is what he becomes
He is what he makes of himself.
'Is he good, is he bad?'
Finally
the reply will be provided
only at the very end
of the performance.

14th July 1789, crowd scene

History is an engraving hung in a classroom.
The Bastille takes up most of the scene,
a huge citadel crowned with battlements
the crenulated stone crown on the head of royalty
which from the height of its towers spiked with guns
and through the dark eyes of its assassins
surveys the crowd below, little men shifting about
pushing cannon and brandishing pikes
their arms outstretched, in a fit pose for posterity,
in tricolore suits, striped trousers, jackets with tails
and their heads, tricornes of boiled leather, scarves
        or bonnets phrygiens...
The smoke from the cannon makes elegant wreaths
and the sky is such a delicate blue you'd think it was
        a velvet suit.
Here and there a stretch of explosive yellow and red
the final spit of scarlet blood diluted in water
and everything must stay like this frozen on the wall
and in memory so the Revolution can remain dutifully tidy
        in the drawers of history
so it can be sold stone by stone
like citizen Pallois who having been given
        the contract
for demolition
sold the bricks of the Bastille
as patriotic souvenirs
(thus confirming the middle-class nature of the event)
– Thanks to which Pallois
became rich before dying in poverty.
What hasn't been said about the storming of the Bastille
        to reduce it to the level
of a silly design on a china plate?
That it was without importance, that there were only, at the
        time
seven inmates in the royal prison
and in any case, half were mad,
and that it isn't by storming Bastilles

by whipping up violent upheavals
late in the day or at dawn
that the world is changed;
that it takes time, patience and lots of skill,
above all skill
(so only those in high places and who share with the
            experts
the art of governance, the wherewithal and good
            manners
can change the world).
Nor is this false.
it does take time
(the middle-class itself needed at least a century)
and yet
without the entry of the people on the scene
without the arrival of the lower orders on the streets
without their tumult of pikes and raised fists
without the scuffle amongst those storming a ghost prison,
who would have given the decisive push of the shoulder against
            the monotonous heap of days?
Who would have brought low the old edifice and built anew a world
without bewigged judges, aristocrats and kings?
Who could have freed the birds of thought, the dream of universal rights,
            of equality and fraternity
from their cages?
Without the brutal arrival of the people on the scene
who could have made the entire house of cards fall into the stream
or dug the wheels of the chariot of history
            out of the pothole?
Who could have given the planet's orbit an entirely different
            pace?

The Saint-Denis Basilica

During the Revolution, the lower orders
having no respect for the sleep of the great
invaded the Saint Denis Basilica
where kings slumber.
They exhumed their skeletons
and threw them in a common grave
so that for once at least
kings and queens
would mix with the common folk of France.
Under the Restoration, Church and State
decided to re-establish in death the divine and eternal order
flouted by sacrilege
and with devotion and care
they reassembled the bones in the crypt.
But have no fear,
despite their scruples,
the bones of royals were mixed
henceforth
with those of the hoi-polloi.

The death of the Incorruptible

He wore little round glasses,
But he was perhaps of all the revolutionaries, the most
        far-sighted.
Behind his distinguished and delicate ways, he was inflexible.
He was no orator, his voice was weak and passionless
But could command the winds,
Enflame the hearts of the patriots and freeze
        The pusillanimous.
His extreme rigour, his sense of Virtue and Justice
Made him a man to love or hate.

He who was against the death penalty
voted for king to be guillotined.
'I regret to declare this fatal truth,' he declared before the Assembly,
'But Louis must die so the homeland may live.'
He spoke for universal suffrage
the end of colonies, civil liberties for Jews and actors
and against monopolists, profiteers,
those who hoard grain
who starve patriots
and put the homeland in danger.

An Idealist who dreamed the Nation would be One
under the gaze of the Supreme Being,
without indulgence for the greedy,
He who was the steady hand of the middle-class Revolution
never had the full support of the middle-classes.
To be incorruptible and to preach virtue
in the midst of a middle-class revolution, is to be suspect.
Whoever doesn't allow himself to be bought can't be fully
            human
(In contrast to Danton, who was always willing to
            do a deal.
Danton who Maximilien could never deal with;
Danton his friend,
his older brother in enmity, who in the end he put an end to).

'Wherever justice does not prevail,' he wrote
the people have exchanged one set of chains for another
but not altered their destiny.'
'I was born to fight crime
not to govern,'
he said in his last message to the Assembly.

He wanted to lay down the law
on prices and incomes
and set the middle-classes and the workers
against him.
It was the passing alliance of the *Plaine*
and the ultra-terrorists which brought him down.

Arrested by the Convention, then set free by the Parisian
            Sections
he refused to go to the City Hall
and to appeal to the three thousand armed common folk
awaiting, on Place de Grève, a sign from him.

(Perhaps he knew, the revolution ice-bound,
the dream was coming to an end…
The time wasn't right for the reign of Justice.
The recourse to Terror wasn't enough
to purify what had become corrupt.)

He, the pure, the incorruptible
had his jaw blown away by a pistol shot
from the policeman Merda
and his head cut off
by the executioner Sanson.

(After his death
in his room they found
the salary cheques for the past two months
he hadn't bothered to cash.)

Evocation of Jean-Paul Marat

Stretched out in my bath, I think of Marat
(his neck bent
like a rabbit in a stew pot,
a most painful position)
his skin disease and his itching
(successful launch of the Ariane rocket
a bus overturned and 100 dead in Karachi)
which towards the end forced him
to spend entire days in the bath
(world news lands on the bubbles).
A young man in Neufchatel, from an immigrant family,
scientifically minded
fighting the Academy
(his enemies today hold against him
his defence of igneous fluid)
he was responsible for astute studies on the use
of electricity in medicine.
He had some happy times
and was ruined.
He lived in London and developed his ideas.
Author of *The Adventures of Count Potowski*
he published from exile: *The Chains of Slavery*.
'I came to the Revolution'
he said, 'with my ideas worked out.'
Marat, the theorist of Insurrection
Forced into hiding during the rule of the Assembly.
Marat in a tunnel
like Diogenes in his barrel
thundering against the King, the Indulgents
and the Deputies in a hurry
to have done with Revolution
Jean-Paul Marat
The People's Friend
The ill-loved
The ill-loved People's Friend.

During the revolutionary days
he brought out
every day and sometimes twice a day
the paper he edited alone.
(Common folk from the provinces and suburbs
Were his propagandists and correspondents).
Truth is a weapon.
Previously journalists have only interpreted the world
it must be changed –

(In the era of the media
the endless stream of pictures and text
drowns sense in words.
Not information but mind formation!)
The Future is becoming bloodless in the blue of the lagoon
Nivea for the bathtub.
Marat the ill-loved will he be forgiven
his sins by publicity?

This arm which hangs out of the bath is mine.
Standing by is the virgin
outraged
a knife in her hand
waxen
her lips reddened
eternally linked to her victim
(a woman in love sings in the shower).

Yesterday the fops threw his ashes into the gutter
once more.
A police dog roams the landing.
It isn't good to be right.

Babeuf, the bloodthirsty

On 23rd July 1789, in a street in Paris,
Citizen Babeuf saw the head of Foulon
(governor of the Bastille) go by on a pike.
Behind him came his son-in-law escorted by the crowd
who promised him the same fate.
Moved by this sight he wrote to his wife:
'Oh! Such painful joy!
I was simultaneously satisfied and unhappy.
I know the people bring justice, I'm in favour of it
when it's achieved by the elimination of the guilty,
but couldn't it now be other than cruel?
Torments of all kinds, quartering, torture, the wheel,
burnings, lashings, hangings, executioners springing up everywhere
have created such bad habits!
The lords, instead of keeping us in order, have made us
    brutal
because that's how they are themselves.
They reap what they have sown...'
– The times certainly have changed
the violence of the lords is no more than a memory
and if the barbarians are still camped at the city gates
in our metropolis, all's quiet
no draughts, nothing smouldering...
In the early evening
The weather forecast predicts no risk of fires.

Inscription for Gracchus Babeuf

In a cage wrapped in wire netting, drawn by horses
hemmed in by armed men, like wild animals
Babeuf and his companions were taken to
    Vendôme.

Son of a poor soldier, François Noël Babeuf
began as an expert in feudal law,
and it was as a lawyer
supposed to defend ancient feudal rights
that in the midst of indecipherable scribble
he discovered the thorn of injustice.

All along the white road which led to Vendôme
men bent to their work in the fields
stood up straight for a moment to watch them pass
and for they who had nothing
those led away were scoundrels...
And the children left their games
to run after them.

Did they know, the onlookers
that their crime was to have conspired
to impose agrarian reform
on the newly privileged
– like the Gracchus brothers, democratic leaders in Rome –
and 'the community of work and property'
sole possible basis of equality?

The court building in Vendôme was being rebuilt
and during the proceedings you could hear the sound of the trowels
because, while they were getting ready to condemn them,
-to avoid being judged by them-
outside, life went on as normal.

When they heard they'd been condemned
Babeuf and Darthé stabbed themselves
– like Marcus Porcius Cato
enemy of Caesar and Pompey-
and their corpses, so they say, were taken to the scaffold.
Because, at that time, anyone who attacked the sacred rights
of property
was robbed of his life
and of his death.

Ode to Toussaint Louverture

Island of devastated streams
surf of down and outs
fleeing of green spume on the sea
in the midst of hillocks and sapodillas
Fatras-Bâton the deformed took up arms
on horseback on l'Oiseau-Tempête
by the guile and glint of the sabre
by courage and trickery
he opens breaches of light
in the enemy's blood.
Raised in his master's hut
he learnt secret words
and foiled the white man's magic.
He was loved and feared, admired and betrayed
then arrested and buried alive
black sun exiled
in snow and cold
in Fort de Joux in the Jura.
And when his island above the sea rose up
to buy his freedom
they had to pay to the former rulers
his weight in gold.
That's how they
took revenge
on him and his fellows.
But in the white, heavy sky of the Tropics
the slaves of the first black Republic
carved in the form of a rainbow
a blue-red opening
which will never close.

Notes on Charles Fourier

Fourier, son of haberdasher; himself a
    shop assistant.
At night by candlelight he writes his work,
mistrusts organisations and doesn't much like the idea
    of revolution.
He wants to be a scientist, a social reformer
and believes he can unravel 'God's laws about industry'.
This well-known dreamer is one of the most astute critics of
    capitalism.
'Poverty,' he wrote, 'makes its appearance in civilization because of
    abundance itself.'
Because 'atomised or civilized industry creates, through its advance,
    the means of happiness, but not happiness.'
'In civilized society, each individual is at war
    with the rest.
In a socialised regime, each individual can find advantage
    only along with society as a whole.'
Admirer of Newton, he tries to found his system on the principle
    of universal attraction
and invents passionate attraction; the free run of desires and
    passions establishing a new harmony…
(Because nothing is done well unless by attraction).
– Later, by the surrealists and some of the rebels of 68,
he was thought of, perhaps wrongly, as a forerunner
of the liberation of desire –
Seized by the sweet madness of taxonomy of concepts,
this subversive was in fact obsessed by order,
a fanatic for tidiness.
In addition: a good psychologist, excellent teacher
and incorrigible innocent.
Every Wednesday, he issued an invitation to dinner
to one of the richest citizens of Paris,
from his up-to-date list
in a restaurant in the Palais royal
hoping one of them would finally agree
to finance his Phalanstery project.
No-one ever turned up.

Flora Tristan visits Lyon

During a tour of France which she undertook
alone – in order to set up the first independent
revolutionary organisation of workers,
Flora Tristan visited the silk workers.
As the police banned any meeting
of more than five
she went into the flats of the Croix-Rousse
which doubled as workshops.
In one of them, the man and woman
wanted to offer her a crown of laurels.
Flora took it, but refusing to keep it for herself
she had it hung on the wall
with a copy of her book
The Union of Workers.
So, it wasn't she
who was honoured
but the ideas she stood for.

Flora Tristan's subscription

Successful writer,
in her book: *The Union Of Workers*
(in her view, her life's work)
Flora Tristan couldn't find a publisher.
So, following the example of the priest
who, through collections, had built the Saint-Sulpice
she could see from her window,
she launched a subscription
modest to begin with,
paid for a several editions,
went on a tour of France
and (in spite of the police on her heels,
the disbelief of many workers,
illness and fatigue,
which, before the end of her journey,
was to wipe her out)
she founded the first
Worker's Union.
From this we can conclude
that faith
can work miracles.
(Or that no great idea
can do without a treasurer.)

The journey to Icaria

I DEPARTURE
Standing on the quay, in black velvet uniforms, they
begin the Song of Departure.
The pilgrims of the future Icaria set off for
the unknown in anxiety and enthusiasm.
They left old Europe in search of
The New World
their hearts full of love and devotion
for the Cause of Humanity.

On 3rd February 1848, the avant-garde left le Havre.
Artisans, painters, carpenters or doctors,
they left behind them a country not ready to
hear the message
of Icarian communism
and of true Christianity.
(Behind them too, they leave those
– lacking the six hundred francs for the journey –
who can't get through Icaria's gates).

In America the news of the revolution
many of them dreamed of taking part in
will catch up with them.

II NAUVOO: THE NEW LIFE
They became familiar with the journey down the Mississippi
songs under the stars in the bright, transparent air
of the March night.
They got to know hunger too, doubt
and dysentery.
In Nauvoo
each couple lived within its bounds ,
everyone had a job.
Meals were taken communally.
Girls and boys went to school together.
On Sunday, adults and children
acted plays.

Sometimes, they went for a picnic
in the meadows near the river.
Amongst them, no money; no-one
getting rich at someone else's expense.
Even jewels were banned
so that inequality, injustice and jealousy
would vanish...
Soon there were four hundred of them.
But the world around them remained
tempting and threatening.

III DEATH OF THE FATHER
They'd dreamt of a sober and fraternal existence
but there is no paradise without abundance.
Men and women wore themselves out with work.
Many fell ill.
Food was sufficient but dull
and life itself became dull.
Alcohol was prohibited
but to survive the community
produced whisky.
To hunt or fish for pleasure
was also forbidden.
The finances grew perilous.
To protect its freedom
the community limited the freedom of its people.
The worst sanction was to be expelled.
But soon, the first defections
began.
And some accused Cabet himself
of encouraging inequality, servility, spying and trickery
by his methods.
The old prophet (who had to be addressed as Papa)
thought only about the happiness of others.
No-one knew better than he
what was good for other people.
When, in the face of growing disorder
divisions and criticism,
he asked for the Constitution to be reviewed
and that greater powers be given him
he was sidelined and expelled by his disciples.

A month later, he died of apoplexy
in Saint-Louis,
on the banks of the Mississippi.

IV THE FALL OF CHELTENHAM
On the Cheltenham farm, six miles away
those who'd stayed faithful
re-established the society.
But they could no longer
shift for themselves.
They went off to town
looking for work,
the children were sent to the local schools,
they had to stop publishing the newspaper
(which, up to that point, they'd refused to give up on)
because life was becoming more and more expensive,
landlords ever more demanding
and creditors less and less patient.
So, Mercadier, the most loyal of the loyal,
suggested the Icarians become capitalists
to save their community.
'We must, he said to them, learn to sell and to make
        a profit.
Up to now, business has been neglected in our community
and it was a big mistake...'
Which, far from saving them, hastened their ruin.
Even Mercadier
gave up.
They say he opened
a fancy goods, gifts and souvenir shop
in Saint-Louis....

V CORNING AND THE COMMUNARDS
In January 1858, the Icarians of Nauvoo
crossed the frozen Mississippi
and pushed westwards
to set themselves up in Corning, Iowa.
When, thirteen years later,
after the Week of Slaughter
a few refugees from the Commune came to join them
still brimming with the ideals of the International

they found a society of peasants
living in honest mediocrity
and voting republican.
Getting along together proved difficult.
Conservatives and radicals
unable to understand each other
finally took their differences
before an American tribunal
which ordered
the dissolution
of the community.

VI SPERANZA AND ADAMS COUNTY
In spite of obstacles and deceit
The Icarians never gave up.
Always, obstinately
they rebuilt their workshops
published their newspapers
practised community of property
and brotherhood.
– Each time a little weaker
each time a little more divided.

On 3rd February 1895
fifty years after the Great Departure
of the Soldiers of Humanity
they were no more than nine
of whom six were over sixty.
At the time of the Assembly
a woman pleaded for New Icaria
to keep going.
No-one listened to her.
Sick, old and tired
unanimously
they voted
for their own end.

VII EPILOGUE
The Icarians who tried to fly
Didn't go too high.
The sun didn't burn them

(their wings simply
weren't good enough
for more than a few clumsy take-offs in a field).

They who hadn't known
socialism in one country
its glory and tragedy
were familiar all the same
with the days of enthusiasm,
discipline and sacrifice,
followed by realism, disillusion
and dereliction.
Today,
mothballed in the hangar of prototypes
in our history's attics
Icarus' wings
wait patiently
for another go.

Blanqui, the Prisoner

By the age of forty-four his hair was white
and he wore threadbare clothes
'a sad ruin dragging a bruised body through the streets'
(as he described himself)
and in this way his renown grew.
To live out his too violent love of liberty
he was condemned to spend
thirty-two years – half of his life – in prison.
Thanks to which he was given the title
'The Prisoner'.
A man of fragile health, he made the State tremble
and the more they persecuted him the further they were from
    their aim.
After four years spent in the depths of a cell
on the Mont Saint-Michel
which rose, black as a scaffold,
its foundations in the mud, above the bay,
he fell ill and was transferred to the prison in Tours.
It was then Louis Philippe
taking account of the prisoner's state
(as well as public opinion)
granted him a pardon.
But the Prisoner refused
asserting his freedom.
(A few years later
in another prison on another hill
– in the Taureau fort in the Bay of Morlaix –
The Conspirator, forced into meditation
became passionate about the stars
and wrote *Eternity According to the Stars*
Then he came back among men,
Their hopes and their prisons).

Blanqui's welcome

Learning of Blanqui's arrival in Bordeaux
where he was expected for a meeting,
the workers left their factories
and came to meet him.
When Blanqui had arrived at the staging post
they untethered the horses
took hold of the harnesses
and pulled him
to the centre of the city.
So, these men
treated as beasts of burden,
in order to honour one of their own
voluntarily
took the place of the animals.

Such a welcome no king could have imagined...
But what revolutionary
should dream of such?

Marx, a caricature

As History teaches us the danger
of lyrical and flattering portraits,
let's try a caricature of Marx
(maybe then someone will buy the poem).
For his enemies, in the very heart of the International
Marx was an intolerable Jew, an insolent
     argumentative character,
an authoritarian and peremptory theoretician
who always wanted the last word
(and – adding insult to injury – usually had it).
In addition
– and can it be forgiven in someone who claims to be the
     liberator of work? –
he was himself a workhorse
a bit like the father of totalitarianism…
It must be said – to drive the point home –
he couldn't always have been easy to live with
even for those closest to him.
Head of a family he was effectively incapable
– due to his revolutionary commitments –
and his passion for study
to guarantee a regular income.
Doting father, he wanted at all costs
good marriages for his daughters
(though they decided otherwise).
A husband always absorbed by his work he didn't mind
     now and again, climbing on the maid
Hélène
(who is buried in the family tomb).
A faithful but demanding and sometimes ungrateful friend
he even managed to annoy for a few months
that modern Pollux, Engels.
Marx, it seems, was all that…

And yet, the mystery remains:
how could such a man
during his lifetime

(and even after his death)
be surrounded by such admiration, affection, friendship
and unflinching loyalty?

Portrait of Marx as Prometheus

In his biography
Franz Mehring compares Marx,
chained to his desk,
prey to carbuncles, lacking money
and still with mountains of questions to be addressed,
working into the early hours
to get *Capital* finished,
to Prometheus, bound to his rock.
He too wanted to steal the fire of knowledge
and put it into man's hands,
he too was accused of the sin of pride,
he too brought down the wrath of Olympus
who even after his death pursued him
with his hatred and his hired men,
because he too was a hero of the struggle for freedom.
But, in his case the tragedy is greater
because if he lived in chains
it wasn't because of a decree from some Hephaestus
but by his own volition.
(And it was to set humanity free
that he enchained himself.)

The League of the Just

In the League of the Just
the shoemaker Bauer, the tailors Lessner and Eccarius,
the miniaturist Pfänder, the clockmaker Moll,
Lochner and a few other
German workers and artisans plotted;
men of good will
who dreamed of establishing
the Kingdom of Justice on earth
(otherwise known as communism).
Marx, who was amongst them,
encouraged them to give up their slogan:
'All men are brothers.'
Because he intended a real struggle for brotherhood.
(Without this first step
which is always taken with difficulty:
recognising that all men aren't brothers,
how can the subsequent steps be taken?)

No doubt, in due course, the slogan had to be restored.

Sketch for a portrait of Bakunin

He called himself a communist, materialist and disciple of Hegel
just like Marx, his brother enemy,
and, just like him, he had a beard.
He wore the tender look of a bear
escaped from a sleepy dream in Siberian exile.
Tireless agitator,
he criss-crossed Europe
to set the spark to the gunpowder dormant in soporific minds.
His speech was clear
his action not always.
Muddle-headed comrade
in Lyon, he provoked an insurrection which was cut short.
After seizing the Town Hall
along with his friends, he proclaimed the abolition of the State
and the beginning of the revolutionary Federation of Communes
then got himself arrested, with two pistols tucked in his belt.
Next he set off for Marseilles and Gênes convinced
– a few months before the setting up of the Paris
Commune –
that France was no longer revolutionary.
Anxious for the freedom of real individuals
he was vigilant against the domination and collusion
of those great abstractions
the State, Science and Religion.
(And he was right).
Always on the alert
incessantly pursued by the police
he never truly finished a book.
And this lack of completion, not due to circumstances,
is perhaps not merely a sign of weakness.
Perhaps it comes also from the refusal
to imprison thought, action and life
in the dogma of a closed system.
(For that too, he remains dear to us).

18th March 1871

It was dawn in the Butte, just as Paris was rousing
when the milkman's churns clink in women's hands
and the carriers go down to the wine merchants,
it was at dawn on the 18th the handiwork was found out.
Making the best of the night,
the commanders sent their troops to occupy the district
and like thieves they seized the cannon.
With their bare hands
They brought from obscure corners of the Butte
Twenty pieces of artillery,
but half-way down
the alarm was raised
the first National Guard gathered at Chateau Rouge
Louise came down, her rifle beneath her coat
and began to shout;
one after another
the women opened their shutters, their windows
and assembled outside in the troubled early-morning air.
Suddenly the tocsin sounded and through the streets
where the drums were beating out the call
the crowds began to stream
from all corners of Montmartre.
Soon the troops were surrounded by men, women and
children in thousands, who overwhelmed them
and prevented them from going forward
a huge, peaceful and threatening crowd
climbing on the cannon, hailing the officers,
fraternising with the soldiers,
a crowd like the sea at high tide,
a stationary swell, noisy and various
a powerful and determined crowd
which, without violence, or almost, took back its cannon.
(In a Marais garden that day
two officers only would be shot).
In the sky the March clouds rolled,
warlike and joyous clouds,
a gentle sun gilded the fraternal mouths of the cannon.

Without planning and by a simple movement
of self-defence
                    the people had risen in revolution.
And the members of the Central Committee,
out of their beds,
came to meet the new masters of the city.
Mars had appeared in the heart of Paris
and he turned the sun-drenched heads
of the terrible and the pacific
(beginning are often terrible and pacific)
Like the giant wheels of a flower-strewn chariot.
The clouds rose over the Butte's shoulder
and hurried down to meet the procession of victors
on the way back up
hauling their trophies.
Thiers and his crowd decamped and hid at Versailles.
Paris imprisoned,
Paris besieged
was going to give to the world
the example of freedom.
Paris, victor today and tomorrow martyred
was going to bequeath to the world
the dream of the socialist republic of free citizens
the great fraternal Federation of communes.

Varlin's watch

for Jacques Gaucheron

In the streets of Paris the heart beats thirteen to the dozen
the cobbles are black, treacherous and slippery.
It's the stalking hour, the time of crime and blood
the time to hide if you're innocent.
Paris is no longer itself and people are strangers,
suddenly doors and shutters slam,
alleyways shut like mousetraps,
air vents become hidden traps
where, head first, bodies
tumble into the abyss.

In the parks
on the squares, at crossroads,
gather dirty herds
the haggard flock of the defeated.

On every street corner people are stopped and killed.
After the great dread, anger is unleashed
to the fury of those who fear it.

The hands of the clock
on the living-room sideboard
are scissor blades
bayonets, knives.

Men, women and children
it's time for arrests, spatchcock executions,
time for counsels of war,
time for deportations.

It's time for the knackers to sharpen their knives
in La Roquette, the Luxembourg, the Parc Monceau,
in Montparnasse, Vincennes, Père Lachaise
the massacres bring sickness unto death,
they execute in thousands
throw bodies into quick lime

and neither the survivors
nor the earth
can take any more
death and blood.

All the gardens are slaughter-houses
The casemates of castles are turned into crematoria.
(Only the fear of epidemics will put an end to the carnage).

On the last barricades or on a street corner
Dombrowski, Rigault, Ferré,
Delescluze, Rossel,
Flourens, Millière and Vermorel
and so many more, foreigners and French,
thrown together in struggle for the betrayed homeland
and for freedom
fall, their arms and their hearts entwined.

Varlin, hurrying, comes down the street
with his fine prophet's head
a soft beard, a serene gaze,
Varlin the trade unionist, the instigator of strikes,
Varlin the bookbinder who wanted all workers
to be able to read and to improve their minds,
Varlin who set up restaurants of solidarity,
in charge of finances and rations for the Commune,
Varlin of the International
responsible for relations between nations,
Varlin trying to escape
is recognised by a priest and denounced.

Carrying out the stations of the cross a group of zealots
seize and lynch him.

His lovely head where worker bees buzzed
with fraternal thoughts is now a destroyed hive.
An eye hangs from its socket.

They stand him against a wall and finish him off.

('We've rid ourselves of socialism'
Thiers will say, relieved. He was wrong.)

They say the officer who had him shot,
(a defender of order and property)
as a souvenir, stole the watch
the workers had given him.

He took away the watch
but he couldn't stop time.
The hands will continue to turn
and one day
the hour of Varlin's dream
will strike.

Marx's tomb

When I woke up in front of Marx's tomb
he asked me how things were going in the world.
(The fog was lifting from the paths of Highgate
a clear sky was opening up over London).
Not too fond – as a materialist –
of talking to the dead
I was ready to take off.
But the old man wouldn't hear of it.
I had to tell him…

'Since your death
much water has passed under the world's bridges.
They've moved mountains
and chasms too.
London is no longer the centre of the Empire.
From Moscow to Peking,
people have mounted assaults on palaces.
They've opened great building sites…
But amongst the fighters, some
who called themselves your followers,
have had new palaces built
with towers on which they stood
to watch processions go by
and have themselves applauded
by the people and protected from them.
(The workers have had to put up with blood-stained plaster
hardly built, their house is too small).
As for capitalism, it's had a facelift
in a West Coast clinic
thanks to the skin of the poor's children.
From South to North
decay reappears
beneath the golden tooth
and poverty is as old as ever.'

During my little speech, he didn't say a word
his heavy dark head sitting

– as if decapitated
which doesn't seem to bother him –
on this plinth where, for inscription there is only:
'Workers of all lands unite.'

A powerful head, I said to myself, as hard as rock
the head of a man
not a star fallen from the heavens.

On his death, Engels sent a telegram:

'Humanity has lost a great mind…
The final victory remains certain
but deviations, mistakes
already inevitable
are now going to take greater significance.
And so, we will have to swallow them.'

(If he had known
old Engels
how much stomach that would take!)
At the foot of the tomb a little grass has grown.
It doesn't cover the tomb of a despot.
He wasn't one of the world's leaders.
He never commanded an army.
He never founded an empire or a police State.
A mausoleum was never built in his honour.
He wasn't driven round in a black limousine.

Marx was the sort who didn't drink milk,
a fighter, a grafter
capable of working three or four nights on the trot without
    sleep.
He called a spade a spade and asked useful questions:
Who owns and who produces?
Who manages and who profits?
He penetrated the secret of the new Pharaohs
and that of humanity's self-creation.
He removed the false noses from theories
and from the prophets, their theatrical beards;

ever since, we've known the heaven of ideas
hides backyards and dirty kitchens
where poorly paid angels are kept busy.
He taught that
to be revolutionary
is not to deduce reality from the dream
but to deduce from reality
the necessary dream
and to bring it to fruition.

'Dreamers of the world unite!
The dream is awakened...'

The hawthorn and the thrush

(song for those shot in Fourmies)
for Roger Bordier

It was on the 1st May
The time when love holds sway

On the square a procession
Workers decked in flowers
Provided no concession
Paraded for eight hours

It was such a merry day
And the thrush's song so gay

Maria led the way
Full of childlike pleasure
For the soldiers her bouquet
Her little hawthorn treasure

It was in pretty May
When love so sweet holds sway

In the midst of her fun
Did she think of a gun?
She was just eighteen then…
The youngest only ten.

It was the month when love holds sway
The day the 1st May

The hawthorn flower of May
Upon the rose dripped blood
The thrush and rose then should
Henceforth stand for this day

The time when love holds sway
Returns with the month of May.

Remembering Paul and Laura Lafargue

Shouldn't a revolutionary be more serious?
Perhaps that's what tempted him to try to in vain to
          understand Marx
when they went walking in the afternoon with
          Laura
in the fields of Hampstead,
and Moor as those close to him called him,
despaired of his future son-in-law
and his Latin temperament
saying, for sure,
he would never manage
to arrange for any of his daughters
the security of a bourgeois marriage.

Can a militant worker praise idleness?
Perhaps this is what this unrepentant worker
Paul Lafargue asked himself
locked in his cell at Saint Pélagie
after the executions at Fourmies
when he began to put together
his famous pamphlet: *The Right to Idleness*
in justification of the demand for an eight hour day,
and where he showed
that the entire history of humanity
is the story of the conquest
by the workers
of the right to take it easy.

Can a militant revolutionary take his own life?
no doubt this is the question many who went to the funeral
of Paul and Laura
asked themselves
when they listened to the speeches of Lenin and Longuet.
But they replied long before
when they decided
so as not to see themselves diminished by age

and leading the movement
at seventy
to commit suicide together.
After an evening in a good Parisian restaurant
a trip to the theatre
and a lifetime of struggle, of poverty and happiness
they went back to their little house in Draveil
had their last glass of wine and held hands
then Lafargue (who loved life without question)
injected the wife he loved like life itself, Laura,
with cyanide
and killed himself.
It was the gardener who found them,
two motionless carnations laid out on the soil.

Report on the progress of freedom

When slavery was invented
It was undoubtedly progress
(because rather than making them work
the custom previously
was to eat captives).
When serfdom appeared
it was also an advance
(because slaves
over whom they had the right of life or death
were often half-hearted in their work
and productivity suffered).
In the same way, when serfdom was replaced by taxation
and little by little wage labour was established
it was a great step forward.
Free at last
to sell to any bidder
their arms, their hands, their brains
on the open labour market
men, women and children
could more easily be exploited
by factory owners
and, by their free will, be enchained
in the hulks of industry.
We still have to decide
By what new advance
of freedom
we are going to replace wage labour.

Epitaph for the First World War

The poplars – a blue line of infantry – collapse
      on the horizon
as though mown down by cannon.
Here those are fallen who had scarcely risen, unopened buds,
clumps of crushed men, youth
like good earth broken by a ploughshare,
lives turned over for the sterile work of history.
Poppies and cornflowers, here fell a country's youth
Mingled with that of another.
The edelweiss and the lilac.
Here the earth is held together by hair
Blond hair and brown hair mingled.
In the black Chemin des Dames, those who will have had
      no entitlement to the gentleness of women lie in
      the muddy bed of the trenches
the poppies and the lilacs and their loves
in the slaughterhouse.
So many hopes, so many inventions and poems which
      will never see the light of day
dreams hung on the butcher's hook
while others in the rear hang their smart overcoats on the peg
and go about their little and their big business.
Special promotion: Young soldiers for sale
end of the line – everything must go-stock clearance
surplus men-civilian and military…
these young who believed they were dying for their country
died for deposit boxes.
They fell that others might remain seated
in their armchairs and on their colonies.
Of them only a half-effaced name remains in the village square
on the monument to the dead
the deceiving monument which represents
those who lie in the earth
as if they were rising to the attack
and portrays as victors the vanquished of war.
On the black ploughed field of history their blood nevertheless
has given rise to a scarlet dawn.

Homage to Jean Jaurès

In the Champ de Mars garden
in Montpellier
wood pigeons are cooing

On the grass in the shade of a nettle-tree
two lovers are stretched out

sleeping peacefully.

*

Near Fabre lodge stands
the statue of Jean Jaurès

On the pedestal is engraved one sentence:
'It's by heading to the sea
that the river
        remains faithful to its source.'

*

It's a nice thought...
but often
before reaching the sea
the river gets lost
in the sands of the estuary...

Lenin in prison

At the time of the first Marxist circles
organised amongst the workers of Saint Petersburg
Lenin was arrested and thrown in prison.
To keep in touch with his comrades
he wrote, in invisible ink, made from milk
many letters
which had to be cut into strips
and soaked in tea...
'Today', he wrote to Nadezhda Krupskaya
'I have eaten six inkwells
made from breadcrumbs'.
It was at this time he began to write
The Development of Capitalism in Russia
(because prison is the university of revolutionaries).
Set free, he regretted
not having been there a little longer,
long enough to finish his book.

October 17

On the square are camped the red soldiers
who've refused to make war on the people
in their long coats and motley *shapkas*
they keep warm by stamping their feet and listening to the news
read by young Seriosha from the latest *Iskra*.
Their great rifles are placed upright on the ground beside them,
crossed like ears of wheat (most of them haven't needed
                to shoot yet.
The time of the bloody harvest
along the famished rivers and as far as the frozen shores
against the white bands spreading pogrom
hasn't yet arrived.)
The whole country has come together for peace, bread and land;
in the workshop, amidst the machines, on the bridges of ships or
                in the circus ring.
There is Vassya with his wispy student's beard, a young refugee Christ
                from Dostoyevsky,
Victor, the metalworker, in his leather jacket, who
                always has a story to tell,
good-hearted Sacha, the sailor who plays the accordion,
old Fyodor who rotates his cigarette between his yellow fingers
                and doesn't dare smoke,
Olga, the telephone girl and her friend Tania,
Timur, who has arrived with his delegation from far Asia
and wears an Astrakhan hat.
From Brest to Archangelsk, empire has given way to Federation
and the entire country has become a soviet.
pressed against the others, in the crowd which masses
                and climbs onto the stands
everyone feels they'll never again be alone;
from now on they're part of the huge and muscular body of the proletariat,
one of the avant-garde of the people of the Earth.
From the side of the platform decorated with streamers, you can see
attentive, tense faces, glasses, little beards,
clear, serious eyes, freckles,
        jovial mugs,
a woman's blonde curls falling from her bun,

and, in a corner, a little man sitting with his head uncovered
like the opal globe of an earthly lamp,
taking notes in pencil and hooking his hand round his ear
to make out what his neighbour is saying to him.
The Revolution isn't an attack, a putsch,
like the time of the Parisian clubs
it's everywhere and the people always together.
And that's enough for the earth to suddenly creak on its hinges
and a door to open on an unknown world
where bluish light flashes and orange sparks dance.
(And old Russia no longer knows itself
running like a panicking chicken,
cackling and staggering in zigzags across the village
asleep on its sand heap, between its tender green birches,
its church, its drunkards and its wooden *isbas*

with flowers painted on black lacquer.)
Little sour green apple which rolls and becomes red
turning in the electric fire of the sparks of the future
the Revolution sets off on the world's pathways.
Soon it will be bigger, more round and luminous than the sun
        on the horizon.

Lenin dances

When Lenin learned that the Bolshevik revolution
had held out for seventy-two days,
one more than the Paris Commune,
he came out of the Kremlin and danced in the snow.
No doubt, he didn't imagine,
with the enemy at the gates
and there where he danced while blowing into his hands
that the Union would hold out for seventy-two years
by iron, blood and roses
in the trenches of Stalingrad, on the Asian steppes
orbiting the earth or on a Siberian dam
where twenty year-old girls would go to build the future
and wagons would roll, in the middle of April
on frozen rivers…
He didn't know either that one day the ice would give
under the weight of men
or perhaps that people would get fed up, for a while,
of carrying their dreams at arm's length
and that early one morning
the Union of Soviet Socialist Republics
would disappear.
But that day he had good reason
to dance in the snow.

The emblem

They took to Lenin in his office in Smolny
(a boarding school for girls turned into the Bolshevik's HQ)
a sketch book, full of designs for emblems
for the very young soviet republic.
To symbolise the union of workers and peasants
the artist comrade had drawn
a hammer crossed with a sickle.
And standing erect between them,
a sword which was meant to represent
the determination to defend
– in the spirit of the dictatorship of the proletariat –
the new State of workers, peasants and soldiers.

Lenin,
who was no choirboy,
had the sword removed.
(Ends mustn't be confused with means.)

Lenin and music

When he listened to music
– for example Beethoven's *Appassionata* –
Lenin found himself
(if Romain Rolland's testimony can be trusted)
moved to tears.
'This music is terrible,
– he said to the writer –
it makes you want to cry
and hold people's heads in your hands
when what's needed is to beat them…'

(And that remark, amongst us,
is like a cloud passing over the earth's face.)

A history of saucepans

for Henry Alleg

When people visited Lenin's little place
In the Smolny palace
(during the years of 'the building
of advanced socialism')
the guide never failed to draw attention
to an old saucepan with a hole in it
which had been repaired by a simple rivet.
'Lenin,' he would explain, had refused
to let it be thrown away...'
(another example of his modesty
and sense of economy
– as well no doubt of the weakness at the time
in the mass production of saucepans.)

Since then, of course, many things have changed
and there's been great progress
in the production of pots and kettles.

The present

Having received from the weavers of Klintz
a length of cloth for his birthday
Lenin sent them this telegram:
'Dear comrades,
I thank you from the bottom of my heart
for your good wishes and present.
But I'll tell you a secret:
there's no need to send me presents.
And I'd be grateful if you could spread this secret
as widely as possible
amongst the workers.'

The housing question

After the revolution, Kerensky moved into
Alexander III's apartments.
As for Lenin, he chose a four-roomed house
for himself and his family.
Subsequently,
amongst those who called themselves his followers,
some, who accomplished much smaller feats,
demanded much larger residences.

The statue

Arriving on the square, to the west of Moscow
the visitor could see
the huge statue of Lenin,
his hand raised, as in greeting
well above the heads of men
perhaps to the clouds, the sun, planes…

Difficult to see in this monument
the portly little man in the worker's cap
with crow's feet and an ironic smile,
the revolutionary,
full of life, simple, direct,
the leader
who hated pomp.

'That,' the visitor could say to himself,
'is what you call abstract art.'

Lenin's brain

At the height of the re-establishment
of capitalism in Russia
a doctor was given the right to carry out a post-mortem
on Lenin's brain.

Once done, he declared it was the normal brain
of a normal man.

Thinking he was putting him down
he paid him a compliment.

Tomb for a mausoleum

During his life, he'd organised attacks on palaces
but not so he could live in them –
After his death, despite his last wishes
(and the opinion expressed by his partner)
his comrades built him a Mausoleum
so workers from all over the world
could come and visit him
in long, faithful processions.
In this way, the habits of the Pharaohs
were revived for him,
the sworn enemy of Empires.
And to keep the symbol alive
the Revolution was embalmed.
So, he who believed in no god
became the object of a new cult,
laid out in his dark crypt,
in his suit, small, ginger, his features a bit stretched,
strangely calm, as if about to wake up,
absent and yet still close,
a waxen face surviving death,
sending us out, sick at heart, on the paths of our
        own death
– touching all the same, like a witness
a brother, now a stranger, a kind of Orpheus back from
the Underworld…
That's how it was because communism
conceived by scientific minds
(which placed doubt above all things)
was also a faith and a religion.
Come from the catacombs to change the world,
the religion of communism accomplished miracles,
defied Caesars and built new kingdoms on Earth.
This religion had its saints, its martyrs,
its interrogators , its corrupt popes,
its executioners, its victims,
its revelations and its mysteries
which will survive to speak of its glory,
its collapse and its execution.

Nikolai Bukharin, the treasured child

Round-faced, fine features, the hint of a little beard
the bearing of a young man which contrasts with the jacket
and boots from the time of the revolution and war
        communism
Nikolai Bukharin, one of the most brilliant
        of the Bolsheviks.
'The treasured child of the party' Lenin said of him
who all the same didn't spare his criticisms.
On the left at 18 (cautious about the concessions which had
        to be agreed)
on the right at 25, (taking a stance against
the emergency legislation and preaching concessions,
but always in favour of free discussion).
– Someone who's mistaken today can be right tomorrow.
One of the rare economists in a country where there's
a shortage of everything
(which doesn't ensure rising prices).
From *The political economy of the investor*
to *The ABC of communism*
he tried to understand the laws of change.
amongst the most clear-thinking, in the torment of revolution,
he defined socialism as 'a planned market economy'.

For the time being, he's pouring himself some tea
and preparing his report on the question
of the provision of corn and the alliance with the peasants.
He's more and more anxious about the turn of events.
He becomes flushed, he feels pale and about to faint.
Yesterday, he fought the left opposition, comrades
        Preobrazhensky
and Trotsky, for whom the workers and peasants block
        can't endure,
whose see salvation only in world revolution.

Sharing the objective of socialism in a single country,
on one occasion, he supported Stalin, the wily centrist,
this Koba who has no soft spot for him
(and even once, in a speech, described him as 'steel-faced').

Today, Stalin has taken up again the opposition programme
and he, who opposes the extermination of the kulaks,
finds himself in the opposition, accused of a Trotskyist plot,
isolated, insulted, soon thrown in prison and condemned to death.
He wanted to have done with the Leviathan,
he will be crushed.
In his view, the final goal is beyond doubt
but the years to come will be blacker and more bitter
than the tea he allowed to go cold at the bottom of his cup.
After his death, Larina, his young wife, transferred from camp to
    camp
in order not to crack, learns by heart every word of the
    testament
for the future generations of party leaders:
'Remember, comrades, that on the flag
You carry in your triumphal procession
Towards communism, there's a drop of my blood.'

Notes for a portrait of Rosa Lux

She was mad about botany, literature and drawing
and, without giving up anything, neither love, nor intelligence,
moving from Poland to Germany,
she became a professional revolutionary.
But for her, there was no question of having a career,
unless as an opponent of careerism.

No doubt she dreamed of a peaceful life.
she often felt closer – she said –
to the blue-tit than her comrades…
But to fight against chauvinism and war,
she threw herself into battle,
spoke in smoke-filled rooms
and wrote while under fire.
August Bebel, her comrade and contradictor said of her
she was 'the last man
of German social democracy.'

In her notes on the Russian revolution, put together in prison,
She wrote: 'freedom, is the freedom of whoever doesn't think
        like the government or the party.'
More lucid than most of her contemporaries,
in the restriction of political debate
she saw the cause of a probable
        bureaucratic degeneracy.
But to the end she supported the October revolution.
In disagreement with the uprising of the Spartakist workers,
and knowing the struggle lost in advance
she stuck with it to the end
forever changing her address, writing incessantly,
        fighting
endlessly to defend the living flame of her paper
        Die Rote Fahne.

'We go forward from defeat to defeat.'
she wrote in her last editorial.
A sensitive, luminous and brilliant red,
a tulip plucked in a field of corn
Rosa is a flower that won't fade.

Rosa's revenge

When they came to look for her, on the night of 15th January 1919,
they found her in her room, reading Goethe's Faust
– She too would have needed eternal youth, to bring her
 dreams to fruition,
but her time was counted by others –
With a blow of his rifle butt, a soldier smashed her jaw.
(Thus, even with her executioners
she could converse no more).
We know how, afterwards, she and Karl Liebknecht
were thrown in cars
Karl cut down by a bullet in a Tiergarten alley
then how the Noske's soldiers
dumped Rosa's body in the Landwehrkanal.

'To be good, quite simply. That's what embraces everything
and counts more than intelligence and the claim
to be right.' she wrote in a letter.
Perhaps she'd given up the abstract, ordered
pure and serene world of maths, which she loved so much
to throw herself into the struggles of the world of men
(where order hides the greatest disorder)
driven by a proud desire for goodness?
She thought in any case that in the very heart of battle
It was necessary – in spite of hatred and violence – to try to stay
        good.
Captain Pabst, commander of the Freikorps which came to arrest her
        and the soldier who fired the shot
were never troubled.
Peaceable citizen of the Federal Republic
Pabst died in his bed
in 1970,
– a victor fallen into oblivion –
As for her, the vanquished,
She'll never be forgotten.

Because her political defeat
had produced a moral victory.

The moth

Rosa Luxemburg, in her cell in Wronke
(as pure and contained as a mountain lake).
Early one morning, she found a moth
in a bad way, in the bathroom
(imprisoned too, and flying hither and thither
to escape, it was worn out)
– Outside, fierce repression
the world rocked –
Rosa takes the moth in the palm of her hand,
carries it gently to the window,
finds it a petal
so it can settle and recover and says to it:
'Listen, outside the blackbird is singing,
don't you think you should find your taste for life too..'
Then she laughs at this little speech
made out loud…

But the moth soon came round
staggered a bit

and slowly flew off to freedom.

Naïve song for the Black Sea mutineers

for Léo Figuères

My love, my beauty with rebel hands
Think of your sailor in foreign lands
Refusing to be the watchdog who stands
Guarding over hordes of gold
And happily joins the mutinous bands
Because his love of life is bold

1919 was the year
When instead of a demob
The General Staff, very queer,
Sent to the Crimea on a job
Many a young French swab
Against October red and clear

If your sailor's joined the mutinous fray
It's to hasten on the break of day
My love, my beauty with rebel hands
Think of your sailor in foreign lands

The battleship not far from port
Aims its cannon at the town
But the sailors cut short
The vile action, close it down:
Officers spreading death for sport,
And seize the flotilla for their crown.

My love, my beauty with rebel hands
Think of your sailor in foreign lands
Who to hasten lovely day
Joined, one dawn, the mutinous fray

Jeanne Labourbe, the teacher,
Is on the sailors' side
For justice she's a preacher
Sails with the radical tide
Soon the police will reach her
Blows fall from every side

Think of your sailor far away
Who on the sea has joined the fray
Think of people young or old
Who are as strong as solid gold

Because in spite of sly amazons
In spite of crime and the blockade
In spite of hordes of foreign sons
In spite of typhus, no table laid
In spite of bullets from wrong guns
The victory of October's made.

My love, my beauty with rebel hands
Think of your sailor in foreign lands
Who loving you for mutiny stands
And who they locked in a prison old
Because his love of life was bold
As the people in the dawn's red bands.

Gramsci climbs the hills

for Eduardo Sanguineti

One day,
a communist worker introduced a Calabrian peasant
to comrade Gramsci
who was with them in prison.
They say the peasant was disappointed to see
how puny and deformed
the great man was.
All the same, with his large head and fine features
atop his sickly and suffering body
(which could stand as a metaphor for the intellectual)
Gramsci, in the view of those who got near him,
was in his own way handsome, charming and terribly alive.
Above all he loved to discuss
with comrades, while walking the streets of Florence,
or Turin, his hands behind his back
like an ancient philosopher.
In 1923, he organised an itinerant school
(in order to avoid being attacked by the fascists)
for the young leaders of the new communist party.
For several days, they climbed up and down
the hills above lake Como.
As he walked, Gramsci taught the rudiments
of Marxist theory; dialectic, economics…
anything they came across, a flower, a stone,
was a pretext for digression.
'Everyone is something of a philosopher,' he said,
'but is it better to think as circumstances dictate
(that is, according to the dominant ideas of your group)
or to think for yourself?'
He said too:
'We are the producers of ourselves.'
He insisted, in order to break free of narrow views
and parochialism,
on the need to reach the highest level of
advanced world thought.

That was how the working-class could move from
                the stage of economic corporatism
                to hegemony
and drive the cultural and moral reform
without which there could be no revolution.
To prevent him thinking
Mussolini had him locked in a tomb
but he didn't manage to deprive him of light
nor to prevent that light reaching us.

Philosophy

One day, during the Budapest Commune
at a factory meeting
a worker challenged Lukacs:
'Nothing has changed, he said to him,
just like before, the bosses go around in big cars.'
Lukacs read him his timetable for the day
and said:
'If you want to change places
I'll give you the car.'

After that, he often went about on foot.

Mayakovsky and the revolution's conservatives

During the summer, Volodya, I came to your place
You weren't there, but I got in easily.
I saw the room, very small, which you occupied
in the communal apartment on Serov Street.
It seems nothing had changed:
to look at the pencils, the note-pads and the blotting paper
one would have thought you'd just gone out.
There on the wooden table were the tools you need
to write a poem.
Newspapers, cigarettes and even an umbrella.
I imagine you seated, your thick, sulky lips,
your sombre eyes sunk in their sockets,
sentimental and unhappy as a young pup,
your lad's cap pulled down over your forehead,
you wanted, with all the strength of your desire
the worker, the *mouzhik*, to learn to walk
with a good stride, boots creaking with pleasure
over this patch of earth which is our planet;
so they might be at home amongst the stars
masters and owners, God's equals,
you wanted the heart's sack to grow
to the size of the universe.
That's when you rang the tocsin of words
calling the oppressed, en masse across the world
to the general uprising
for Love, Revolution, hot water
and the Fifth International. Because you knew
that while they sleep,
the Revolution dies. And it's not enough
to have expelled Kings in order to have won.
You, who to move things forward, struggled against restraints
always with the masses and always against them,
you knew that progress doesn't happen
without struggle and contradiction.
Ah, Volodya, my brother…
it's a long time since you came home.

The house has changed a lot,
you wouldn't even recognise the staircase,
the Revolution's Conservatives have it to a mausoleum.
Here, where you lived with your neighbours, with their nippers,
dirty, snotty, as bubbly as a kettle,
they've covered the walls with pink marble
and put all over the place patriotic friezes
with imitation guns brandished brazenly
(strange company for you, these pallid statues,
not made for fighting but for creating shock.)
Those who killed you with a blow from the ace of spades
right in your heart, covered you in naphthalene
and wound round your neck a pioneer's scarf.
Tomorrow, perhaps, in the Court of History
they'll say, checking their voluminous dossier,
'They wanted to save the revolution, they lost it.
They wanted to turn it into a statue, they petrified it.'
But today, Volodya, my friend, my brother
October has come down from its pedestal
revolutionaries are a little lost
but the planet makes its own revolution
and water drips from the end of stalactites.
You, you would have your place amongst us again
to get us pulling together, to cry out loud
frowning cloud, ordinary bloke…
There are still some distinguished poets of course
who would consign you to limbo
with a moist rubber stamp.
Who cares, all we have to do is open one of your books
to be struck by your force.
Your poetry's shoulders are too wide;
they won't fit the doorways
leading to Academies.
Volodya, my friend, I didn't get to meet you
But, in the visitors' book, for you, I left this message:
'If you are taking a stroll
somewhere around the Earth
drop in at home!'

Leon Trotsky, the people's commissar

Leon Davidovitch Bronstein, *aka* Trotsky
(a name given by a prison guard
which suggests a fine sense of contradiction)
wasn't the easiest of companions (and knew little ease).
Sophisticated intellectual
(no doubt one of the most cultured of the lot)
he was responsible for organising
– general without stripes –
an army of several million men, the Red Army,
with political commissars to supervise the former officers.
He was seen, upright, in a leather jacket,
in a compartment of his armoured train
ploughing across the country
to galvanise the poorly equipped red fighters
during the war against the white armies.
He who was often in dispute and would soon be
the very symbol of opposition
(or if you like, the counter-revolution)
was also the iron fist who repressed Makhno's gang
and the sailor's insurrection in Kronstadt.
A comrade whose leanings were sometimes negative
'We have ruined Russia to beat the Whites,'
he said, while the sky turned red, crossed by patches
          of black clouds
like fish, armoured sharks in the evening air,
while typhus and famine rage
and on the borders of the Volga, they record
          instances of cannibalism.
When the time came to confront Stalin,
he who knew the value of the use of force,
refused to rely on the army to foment his own
          18th Brumaire.
But, from the politicization of the army
to the militarization of the Party,
it will be said he contributed to the
construction of the machine which was to devour him,
(and when the revolution turns, it's the machine which
          gains the upper hand...)

At Joffe's funeral (he killed himself)
in front of an assembly of opponents, workers and soldiers,
beneath the first flakes of snow, bare-headed, he made his first
     public speech in Russia.
(He was kept out of the 10th anniversary celebrations of October.)

All the same, in spite of traps and betrayals,
     in spite of crime and paranoia,
and tragedies greater than Shakespeare's,
he was amongst those who allowed the future to be born.
The wind rose on the steppes, the earth's axis went awry,
and the Orient, like a huge bear, from the depths of its lair began
     to move.

Trotsky on Prinkipo

Picked up by the secret police on 18 January
and taken to Alma Ata,
Trotsky was stripped of his Soviet
nationality and sent into exile.
He found refuge on Prinkipo,
the island to which the Great Turk exiled nobles
(after having, sometimes, had their eyes plucked out
because they'd seen too much or were too far-seeing).
And on the stony island, he finds a temporary haven,
a stopping place on the path of exile.
Here, in this moment of enforced exile,
Trotsky fishes for spindle-shaped mackerel,
silver suited, striped with blue and black,
by throwing stones at them, just like the locals.
'If that's how you throw stones at the bourgeoisie,'
he said laughingly to his secretary, 'it's got a long life ahead!'
(Because, in all circumstances, a leader remains a leader…)
Subsequently, it was he who was pursued and hunted,
who had stones thrown at him,
as they went for his ideas, his companions, those close to him
(who, however, were not numerous).
He wrote to his daughter Zina telling her not to join him
whether out of mistrust or to protect her.
(A little later, in Berlin, she killed herself.)
His son Sedov, who was organising the networks of supporters
was killed in Paris by Stalin's agents.
His other son, Sergey, who took no part in politics, died in the
    Lubyanka.
As for him, not content with wiping him out
Stalin tried to wipe out the least trace of him
that might have survived.
Even his picture was erased on official photos.

On the nature of a famous perversion

'Stalinism,' said the philosopher Henri Lefebvre
'is essentially the confusion of a limited understanding
and a limitless power...'
That understanding was lacking
is hardly in doubt
nor that power without limit was abundant.
(Combined effects of the failure of democracy
and the lack of political debate).
But, above all, there was confusion
as in all churches
between power and knowledge
– theocratic deviation –
In this sense, the function of 'general secretary'
at first a subsidiary function and a matter of organisation
created by Stalin, became through Stalin,
(possessor of authority over the Party
because possessor of supreme knowledge)
the supreme function.
He who rules, rules because he knows
and because he rules, he knows
(and that's why – because things always end up like this –
he ended up ignorant of what he should have known
mistaken about himself and betrayed).
The very danger haunting any organisation
Which allows authority to flow from function.
– The problem then is this: to hang on to faith
but to have done with church hierarchy.
– Or rather: to have done with church hierarchy
in order to keep faith alive.

What are communists made of?

In the speech he made at Lenin's funeral
Stalin declared: Communists are
    made of special stuff.'
(It was well said that day as they buried
a man who was going to take his place in History
    in an everyday suit
stunning the world still today by being so different from
    the Tsar
decked out like a puppet in his ponderous clothes embroidered
    with jewels.)
'Communists,' Stalin had said, 'are made of special stuff.'
In this way, in a single sentence, he'd tailored the suit of
    The New Man
cut at one go from select, faultless fabric.
After that, all that remained was to get rid of the old rags,
tinsel of the aged world, men of patches…
'No,' says Moshe the tailor, shaking his head,
'communists are ordinary folk, made,
by and large, from the most commonplace material…'
'But sometimes also from rarer stuff…'
'Perhaps, but it's not the material that makes a communist.'
'What then?' asks the passer-by… 'sharing their overcoat?'
'No, the simple fact of rolling up their sleeves.'

Georgi Dimitrov

for Lubomir Levtchev

After the Reichstag fire
(which gave Europe and the world a warning
of many more fires)
Georgi Dimitrov, secretary of the Comintern
Was captured by the Nazis and thrown in prison.
'I'm going to settle your hash!' Göring said to him.
So he stayed for five months
in solitary confinement
in handcuffs.
(They even confiscated his glasses.)
During this time, to prepare for his trial
and put together his defence
which was to be an indictment,
with no help,
he studied German history.
And the Reichstag flames danced in his night.
But Dimitrov's sky was alive too with anonymous stars
and at night in his cell their light came to him.
All over the world people rose in solidarity:
Papers, poster, tracts were printed.
To denounce the real fire-raisers
a *Brown Book* was published
and a counter-trial organised.
So, when the time for confrontation came,
it was the Nazis themselves who were judged.
and what was intended to be the triumph of their propaganda
was its first defeat.
For this was one of the first victories against them
of courage
and solidarity.

A waltz for the Popular Front

An accordion drowns out the factory's buzz
in their chequered shirts the workers dance.
Through the windows comes the sun's bright glance;
it's a clear new spring and the world's for us.

Let those who work own the factory, the land!
night and day we're here all we need is at hand,
we clean all the tools that are at our command
the bosses will lose for united we stand!

Tomorrow by train or a bike made for two
we'll go for a fortnight away by the sea
throw ourselves in the waves, breath the air fresh and free,
see our France, have a picnic under skies azure blue.

What faces they pull, the bourgeois, the rich
as we set off together, all friends, without hitch
to the sun, to the beaches, to the sand, to the coast
pinch any rocks or sea shells, we're toast!

Sun, culture, science and all that it classes
it's not there preserve, it's for us all then!
Rebels in caps, proles, working lasses,
We've a right to it all, women and men!

Yes, life is ours and we'll enjoy it
though songs and dance only last for a bit,
a bright spell... soon up ahead there sit
threat, fascism, treason, shit.

Spain in blood and jasmine

Spain, land of beaten leather
the men wear scarves round their necks
and carry heavy rifles.
They stamp their feet and blow into their hands
to dispel the cold which comes up from the south
with Franco's troops
Hitler's and Mussolini's planes
the cold of the dark regime
defenders of great wealth
of church and tradition
who to fight against life have taken the slogan
'Long live death!'

The olive groves
silver-tipped look like martyr's bodies
put to the test
but they are woods of justice
of the people's pain.

On the plain, the orange trees
can no longer manage to hold at arm's length
their crucified suns.
O sweet Spain
Spain where the violets sing profoundly
Jasmine Spain
Spain of forged iron and wild mint
Spain of Federico, of Miguel of Rafael
Spain of poets and goatherds...
Hope has been yours all the same
the wagons draped with red flags
crossing the river's dry bed
the hills and the valleys
with scarlet songs
and bursts of laughter.
You've known the living water of youth drunk in festivity
the great sensitive drum of brotherhood
the warm friendship of peoples;

primary school teachers, workers, students
who left their homes
to fly to the aid of the republic.

Spain you had become the homeland of common folk
the motherland of workers the world over.

You were beaten by the weapons of Franco, Hitler,
Mussolini
by the non-intervention of haughty democracies
    and by your own divisions.
You lost your blood on the way
you were abandoned in the ditch
like the carcass of a mule.

Spain of the barbed wire years
Spain of the dove locked in the confessional
Spain of pride cast to the winds
in the midst of tourists
like a cow-boy's hat
during the *corrida*
Spain you've left us the memory of a people
and the gesture of the Brigades
the unprecedented epic
of volunteer soldiers
the gesture of international solidarity
humanity suddenly conscious of itself.

On your injured flags you will retain forever
the sun of dignity
the blood of revolt
and your deep, purple pain.

But the people aren't a bull in a ring.
you can stick swords in their back
make red tulips of blood spurt
against the ink-black night of their spine
you can make them kneel on the ground
you can stab them and bury
a sword between their eyes

but you'll never kill them
because even when driven down, beaten, martyred
the people will always rise
and sometimes, they even
gore the executioners dressed in costumes of light
who dance on their sorrow.

The browns and the reds

The Nazis too put red on their flags.
They spoke of socialism and revolution
in their speeches (shouted into microphones
from platforms at huge meetings).
They too denounced the plutocrats from time to time.
They too called for the building of a new world
a new order, a new man...
They too exalted work, youth, sport
and the fraternity of fighters...
They too walked shoulder to shoulder, chanting.

But for them, violence was an end in itself
and if they walked together
it quickly became as assassins
united by their common complicity in crime
and not in the hope of the song of days to come.
And if they put red on their flags
it was the better to defeat socialism
and revolution.

Willi Münzenberg

This man, with the good, jovial smile of a Thuringian workman,
who could be taken for a sales rep
with his leather briefcase in his hand,
was a commercial traveller of the Revolution.
According to his 'biog' (which we haven't managed to put together
    completely)
this man of the shadows devoted his life to enlightening
public opinion.
Red eminence, as his enemies called him,
he didn't pursue honours and medals
but served his class.
He worked with everybody.
His 'fellow travellers' were:
Brecht, Heartfield, Barbusse, Koestler, Gide or Romain
    Rolland.
Convinced revolutionary
he understood it wasn't enough to be right
and that the most upright ideas must be the strongest.
Fighting capital,
with his newspapers, his publishing houses,
his photo agencies and his films,
he built a potent *konzern*.
Supreme propagandist
He knew propaganda can't do everything.
A Party man, he acted without bothering about bureaucrats.
To the end, he had Lenin's support;
But his confidence in Stalin wasn't exactly long-lasting.
Fleeing before the advance of German troops
it was near Lyon he died
hung from a branch…
– Leaning on the Party, he could act as he saw fit
and that's why he was so effective.
– But it's because he was so effective
and useful to the Party that
unable to put up with him acting according to his lights
it withdrew its support.
– A difficult dialectical point.
– Say rather: our best dialecticians
did not always tolerate dialectics.

Hans, the Hamburg docker

for Gerhard Leo

When the Nazis came to get him from jail
to shoot him, Hans the Hamburg docker
was asked, as they knew the formalities,
what his final wish would be.

In the early morning mist,
the cranes overlooking the port
stretch out their arms like despairing mothers.

– I'd like to have my hands free
replied Hans, the communist docker
arrested for distributing tracts against the war
on the quayside.

For a moment, the executioners hesitated.
(To smoke a final cigarette or drink a last brandy
there's no need to have your hands untied.)
But at least he wouldn't be able to escape.

In the early morning mist
the cranes are black and lonely
in the cold on the Hamburg docks
like powerless and despairing mothers.

Then, just for a moment, they agreed to take off
        his binds;
Hans didn't thank them.
He loosened his fingers
looked the officer in the eyes
and with his closed, heavy, hard fist
like the metal hook hanging from the crane overhead
punched him
full in the face.

Naturally, this didn't change the course of the war
and Hans, the docker, was shot on the spot
but at least he'd fought till the end.

And when, coming out of the mist, in the early morning,
in the port of Hamburg
his comrades started their shift,
their fists closed in their pockets,
it seemed to them that these great cranes, black, solid and
        lonely
would soon make perfect gallows.

Jean-Pierre Timbaud

He was called Timbaud – 'Tintin' to his friends –
(He never dreamed he'd be a hero).
He was a metalworker, a Parisian street lad
Plump, a pipe in his mouth and always a ready wit
And pulled down on his head a worker's cap
– He was forever busy.

He was called Timbaud – 'Tintin' to his mates –
he trained as a caster
at Rudier's who cast for the great sculptors.
Metalworker artist he forged for Rodin
and then, trade unionist, he soon made it his desire
to bring together all the Parisian metalworkers.

He never dreamed he'd end up a hero
all the same he was. Clear-thinking busy men,
the kind the Nazis chose for hostages
but who were stronger than their executioners.
To his wife and daughter, to give them courage
when the time to die came, he wrote:

'I shall be shot in a few minutes.
But, my dear, my hands don't tremble…' and then
'you will see my dream realised, my death
Will have been some use…' and then, in front of
the German firing squad
he let out this cry – astonishing to some –
'Long live the KPD!'

He was called Timbaud – 'Tintin' to his mates –
(he'd never dreamed he'd be a hero)
He was one of the twenty-seven of Chateaubriant
shot by the Nazis, in a gravel-pit,
twenty-seven, a flash of blue sky between their teeth,
twenty-seven, who died singing, who falling, rose
and made new fighters rise.

Ballad of the francs-tireurs and partisans

The francs-tireurs hide in the foliage
of the elms and chestnut trees
they blend with the narrow trunks
of the oaks and holly-oaks

They rustle with the wind
They run with the torrent
Grow like the grass
Make sparks fly

Pierre-bond-breaker
Claire-of the fountains
Jean-wall leaper
Louis-wild wind

A ruin will do for shelter
A hut is their palace
Every encounter an adventure
And rest a memory

They carry suitcases
weapons, secrets
words, tracts
hidden messages

Leon-the strong
Max- the chemist
Paul-of the planes
Lea- the flame

The francs-tireurs blend
with the earth's heart-beat
the breathing of plants
the bustle of towns.

They disappear into the shadows
hide in the light
fall on a corner
get up in the morning

José-the mad
Jeanne-winged feet
Ange-iron hands
Lucie-the star

They're here and elsewhere
Their day is born of night
No longer having a country
They discover a homeland.

So the song of those who lost their names
Writes itself
They who smuggled hope
And whose first name was Freedom.

An icon from wartime

Everyone had warned him, but he didn't want
    to believe the reports,
nor the generals, nor the western chancelleries
nor his own services,
not even Sorge, the most talented of his secret agents.
Now Hitler's troops, all along
    the front,
overthrow a poorly prepared and equipped Red Army.
The Germans are at the gates of Moscow.
Since the end of the summer, the town has started to empty
(the Union's government has retreated to
    Kuibyshev).
Everyone who can heads for the station
to go east.
That's when Stalin appears
In an old Packard convertible
Going through the town in the opposite direction.
To give the signal for the counter-attack
he'd gone to the front: in the street
(there – like every day – stand the people).

The flag on the Reichstag

'It's a photo known all over the world'
he says (he who hardly travels any more).
The young Red Army soldier stands on the Reichstag
In his hand he holds the pole of the huge red flag
with its hammer, sickle and star
which he sets up over burning Berlin
and the flag is a flame
this flag is the flaming heart of the people
who during four years under the jackboot
had hoped for victory.
This photo, they tell us, has a history.
It's the work of Yevgeny Khaldei,
a TASS agency photographer.
When Berlin was about to fall
he was sent to the battlefield
– like they used to do with painters –
so he could take the photo
which would immortalise this moment.
Before leaving, as he needed a flag,
he asked the senior officer
for three big regimental tablecloths
drew the emblems himself and sewed them on
then went to Berlin.
From all sides surged men who were heading
to the centre.
The Fifth Regiment and the shock troops of the Eighth
advanced under fire, smoke and disorder...
At the foot of the Reichstag, he met three soldiers
and took them with him to the top.
Beneath them the cupola is on fire.
they find a length of wood which will do for a pole
and choose the right angle for the shot;
they need to get yet higher
above the emptiness.
'I'll go, if someone will hold my legs,'
a soldier agrees.
They're there, now to set up the clichéd image:

the flag unfurled and waving in the wind
and the town visible beneath.
That's it!
When the picture arrives in the Moscow office
'What have you done!' his boss asks
'this soldier is wearing a watch on each wrist
he's a thief…'
So, to rescue his photo
and the honour of the Red Army
Yevgeny takes a needle
and scratches his film.
Thus, the retouched photo entered history
(history which itself is retouched…)

But the real story of this photo
is that to take it there had to be
twenty million deaths
so the soldier's legs could be held above the void,
twenty million deaths
entire peoples on the move day and night,
courage and discipline
and the determination of those who think
the future belongs to them
and sometimes heroes who behave like thieves
or thieves like heroes.

But on the day of victory
what do shadows in the picture matter?

Afterwards, Yevgeny went on
photographing communism
and its victories
rather than the shadows in pictures.
'I didn't take pictures of the queues,' he said,
a temporary problem which was going to sort itself out
life was going to be better…
In 1958, he was sacked,
the photographer of the Soviet Union's victory
the militant communist
because he was a Jew;
the shadows in the picture caught up with him.

But, born the same year as the revolution
he still believed in its light
and to his final breath
he goes on hoping.

Today Yevgeny
walks in the shadows
in the picture climbs with difficulty
an endless stairway. But still a joker,
he bullies the cameraman from German tv
accusing him of wanting to make him look,
out of breath,
to please the audience.

Man, the most precious capital

'Man is the most precious capital,'
he liked to say
and that was thought of
as a new definition of humanism
But the tree that shoots up in the forest
does it do so
to create good planks?

(The individual reduced to a factor of production:
the capitalist's dream
that communists have sometimes excelled them in.)
It has to be said that the time
was prone to see in the forest nothing but timber
because the lag in productivity
had to be overcome.

But little by little, we are leaving behind this phase of human life
where man, instead of being his own end,
is a means.

Canvas for a tragedy

The greater his power over things,
the oceans of wheat,
the mountains of tractors,
the rivers of steel,
the more he felt the ranks thinning out around him
and in himself the paths through which light might enter
grew darker
because little by little his confidence in men weakened…
The more his success multiplied
in building socialism
the more efficient the machine became
the more united the masses
the greater his preoccupation with defeat…
Reports noted rumours, sly criticisms
even collusion with the enemy
sometimes amongst the most faithful companions.
The world was filled with traitors, deaths
and conspiracies.
The closest to him, one by one
defected.
Comrade Nadya Alliluyeva, his wife,
she too – by killing herself – deserted the struggle
and from this dereliction he never recovered.
He said to himself he should have been more attentive to her
but he had so much to do… so much
to build and defend the soviet State,
the construction of heavy industry,
the mechanisation of farming
and he knew there was a heavy price to pay.
'To work for common happiness
left him no leisure
to worry about individual unhappiness.'

Report on a little screw

Ease of expression returned to Stalin
who, on the eve of War, at a reception
raised his glass and proposed a toast
'to the simple, ordinary, modest folk, the *'little screws'*
who keep our huge engine of State running,
their name is legion...' and the entire press quoted him.
During the years of the great effort of construction,
on the building sites of the Urals or the ports of Yang Tse,
or Stakhanov in Lei Feng,
in their millions, men and women could be proud
and stand tall, to know they were just 'little screws'

in the construction of State Socialism.
(An heroic time, a tragic time, when, to hold firm
men of steel tightened the bolts.)
– *A mechanistic view, outmoded today*
in a world of microprocessors and biochemistry –

All the same, men and women in their millions…

Story of a lie

The big house always had to be tidy.
He could never leave his toys on the floor
climb on the armchairs, play with the tv
without permission,
put his fingers in the jam,
show his willy to his little cousin,
mess around with the electric sockets,
or lean out of the window.
That (and other things too)
his parents forbade
in the best interest of the children.
And if they messed about
they were shut in the dark beneath the stairs
and the bogeyman would look after the key.
As a matter of fact, everything went fairly well,
it was a happy house
(a house where happiness was obligatory)
a house without history
where parents and children never fell out
(because people and Party were one).
But soon, the children began
to lie to their parents
so they would hear what they wanted to hear.
Sometimes, they even believed their own lies.
As for the bosses, not always gullible,
they adjusted to these lies
which were necessary to keep things in order.
Besides, they didn't always tell the truth
to the people (so as not to worry them
or because they didn't know it.)
It worked for a while…
(Then along came adolescence.)

Report on the death of Lev Davidovitch

He had to become part of the immediate circle.
So it was decided he'd take as a lover,
or even fiancé, Sylvia, a regular visitor to the exile's house.
Every day he gets letters from all over the world,
piles up clipping from the press, dictates his letters.
For the Dewey Commission, he's dug out all his old files,
in the event of an international trial which will acquit him
of all accusations.
Like a lawyer, he pursues his political case
there being nothing but his honour left to defend
(his comrades are scattered all over the world,
in prison, or have given up the fight.)
Maybe now and again Mercader
holds the outcast in esteem.
Cardenas's government has given the land to the peasants
but he has little contact with the Mexicans –
he's still interested in art (his relations with
    Diego Rivera and Frida Kahlo are friendly) –
In the Manifesto *Surrealism In The Service of Revolution*
– put together during André Breton's visit – he's the one
who insisted on the sentence giving total freedom to art.
In the garden, the agaves are getting dusty.
His two sons and his daughter are already dead,
the entire family will be decimated.
A tragedy worthy of the Greeks…
are the heads of assassins always drenched in blood?
Beneath the Mexican sun the Siberian cold has caught up with him.
When M took the ice-axe from under his jacket
and put it to T's head
the idea was to smash the opposition's skull.
The order was carried out to the letter.
Later, the report's author would be made a Soviet hero
and buried in the Kremlin.

They thought they were saving the revolution: they sent it awry.
By destroying a man's brain
it was the spirit of the revolution they fatally wounded
and also its heart.

Letter to comrade Brecht on the uses of goodness

(in response to certain tittle-tattle recently spread about him)

I
The playwright sits in an armchair
by a lake, somewhere in the north
while in the south war rages.
He wears a grey jumper and is smiling,
in his mouth, a cigar, in his hand, a glass of schnapps;
next to him two white-fleshed, comely girls
run naked on the diving-board and jump,
laughing, into the water.
So, the commentator says, the revolutionary writer
was nothing but a selfish playboy
who made use of his female comrades.
All the same, he who does himself a bit of good
while doing good to others
deserves to be thought of
as good.
And can anyone who disdains a good life
fight for a better one?

II
Appearing before
the House Un-American Activities Committee,
the dialectician
(who knew in certain circumstances
pushing contradiction gets you nowhere)
declared – true enough –
that he'd never been a member of the Communist Party.
Before a stronger enemy
stupidity being the best defence
of intelligent people
he used trickery, the power of the weak.
So, the man of dialectic, says the commentator,
not satisfied with being a Marxist, was a coward
and a poor comrade.
But does goodness reside in handing yourself over
bound hand and foot to your enemy?

III
After the war, the supporter of Grand Theory
chose the GDR,
but got himself an Austrian passport.
(You can never be too careful about your friends.)
When the workers marched down the Unter den Linden
on the way to Alexanderplatz
protesting against workers' power.
he suggested arming the workers
to uphold the power they were fighting against.
Which just goes to show, says the commentator,
his ambivalence and his compromise.
But how can a new order be built
without educating the people
and being educated by them?
In his view, popular sovereignty
meant the sovereignty of arguments.
(Not always an easy position.)
But rather than the comfort of a moral position
the moralist preferred the discomfort of politics.
P.S.
You dreamed, old comrade
of the world turned into a theatre
where everyone could watch the play
through cigar smoke
and discuss the production.
A theatre in which the audience
would become not merely the actors
but also the authors.
You said, old comrade, that in this world
where doing good is often dangerous
it isn't enough to be good
the world must be made better.
You helped us guard against
the ever-present threat of holier-than-thouism.
The risk – you always knew
but since then we've seen it confirmed –
was cynicism.
That's why
you who taught the hard laws of class struggle

and weren't by all accounts too holy
thought of kindness as the supreme quality.
That's also why
you remain necessary.

Odyssey of the New Man

I
The New Man they said was on the way never
    got here.
The order was cancelled.
Still, we met him more than once.
He wore a steel worker's helmet
it's peak pushed up on his forehead
his gaze was steady and clear.
His fist was firmly closed
on a shovel:
he was fulfilling the plan.
– Of course, he'd left his joker's rebellious irony
in the changing room –
But for the first time in the history of the world
statues were raised to him, the worker,
instead of to generals.
Today, his dismantled statue lies overturned in the park,
half hidden by the snow
as old men go by, baskets in their hands,
those who struggle to get by,
those who deal drugs.

II
Sometimes,
when the New Man didn't show,
they made the old ones disappear.
(But still the New Man didn't arrive.)
Because often in this century materialists
showed themselves capable of
criminal idealism.

III
All the same, in the century we often saw
       old men reveal a new way of thinking
       struggle for themselves and others
       with self-sacrifice
       carry out feats, volunteer,

work for no reward,
teach and learn,
be joyful and determined
help one another
be capable of internationalism
enthusiasm and courage.
(Can you blame us for believing in the arrival of the New Man?)

IV
But the New Man they promised didn't come
We were waiting but the order was cancelled.
He hadn't had enough to eat.
He needed shoes.
His home was too small...
And no doubt he wasn't free
to travel.
You see the New Man needs his home comforts...

V
In his day, Marx never spoke
of the New Man.
He confined himself to talking about
the Whole man.

However you look at it
on the street in your own house
ours is the time of unfinished men.
Some have the heart missing,
others the brain or the hand....

The New Man
of the time just passed
he too
was incomplete.

(Like a saint)

We know he had a heart, hands
often even a brain.
But what did he do with his tongue?

And did he have genitals?
We may as well ask.

When the era of mutilated men comes to an end
men and women who've been unfinished forever
will round themselves off.
Imperfect
together they'll head
towards a little more perfection.

Metamorphosis of the human forest

We don't dream of a forest
where all the trees will be the same size.
(But that the earth will be the same for everyone
and they can all grow
and that in the undergrowth
the plants are blotted out by the tall trees
that no-one will live to anyone else's detriment
and that no-one will be condemned
to be a sickly bush.)
We don't dream of a forest
where only one kind of tree will grow.
We don't dream, of a forest of dwarf trees
(but of being able to say of great men,
something hardly likely today,
'He was of real use to others.')
We don't dream of an abandoned forest
which grows wild and dark
taken over by roots and brush.
We don't dream of an orderly forest
set out in straight lines.
We dream of a forest which lives and breathes
a forest all will care for
a forest grown for the usefulness of its wood
and the pleasure of walking there.
Because what creates the beauty of a forest
is the vitality of its trees
their unity and diversity
their mingled odours
the force of the sap
of what dies and what is born.
What creates the beauty of the forest
is the cheeky cry of the jay
the flash of the playful squirrel
the lovely sway of the ferns,
what makes for the beauty of the forest
are the pathways and the clearings
and the daylight striking through the foliage.

The dove of peace

for Pierre Gamara

This is how symbols are born:
one day Picasso picked up his pencils
and drew a pigeon,
a very ordinary bird,
well-known but not domestic,
which lives among people in big cities
and isn't usually well thought of.
Then, the drawing done,
he picked up his telephone and called the Peace Movement.
A young militant called Pierre
(who would later become a poet and novelist)
came to his door
then went off into Paris
the pigeon under his arm.
A little later, the bird took off
and flew round the world
turning itself into
the Dove of Peace.

The portrait of Stalin

for Roger Somville

When Stalin died, Picasso drew his portrait
and the picture,
published on the front page of *Lettres françaises*
caused a kerfuffle.
Lots of radicals sent letters of protest
and the Party leadership asked Aragon,
who ran the magazine, to take himself to task.
Picasso, however,
paying no attention to official portraits of
'The little father of the people'
and the great conquering war hero
had done no more than render Stalin
in his own way
showing him as a young trainee priest
and the bank-robbing Georgian revolutionary he was
with serious eyes and a heavy moustache.
And this flattering portrait was taken as blasphemy.
Was it because Picasso, a revolutionary painter,
tore the death mask from death itself
and brought a touch of life to the mourning?
Or maybe because beneath the young man's face
the dictator's anger was already visible?
Then again, perhaps because by painting him so young
Picasso depicted an unrealised dream,
an iconic view of revolution
when everything was still possible?

Earl Browder

(an attempt to put together a biog)
for Jack Hirschman

According to what we know, Browder's case isn't simple.
Born in Wichita in 1891, in a family of seven children
studied business
worked as a cashier for the Wallenstein & Cohn Dry Goods Co
then as an accountant for the Potts Drug Company.
According to his fellow office workers
he was a straight guy and a good friend
a model and efficient employee
(too bad his political ideas made a mess of his career.)
He came early to socialism (under the influence of his father, a
    primary teacher)
joined the young communists and, with his sister
        Marguerite,
lived in Moscow for two years to train himself.
A leading light in the International
he was also sent to Shanghai for three years
at the head of the Pan Pacific union
to help get the movement going in China.
(there too he seems to have been well thought of.)
Back in the United States, his supporters put him forward
        in several elections.
He stood for the presidency in 1936.
(His activism got him imprisoned four times
for conscientious objection, use of false papers and outrage to the Senate
– even then a certain senator McCarthy was involved.)
In spite of being hounded by the extreme right
he found a place in the American political system.
Faced with the 'Wall Street Gang' and the fascists of the Liberty League
he proposed the union of democrats and support for Roosevelt.
After the Teheran Conference (Churchill, Stalin and Roosevelt together)
he thought people had entered a 'new world'
(even back then the times were new…)
In the name of the struggle for peace, the class struggle should be altered.
'If you want to call the kind of capitalism which exists in the United
    States

the system of the freedom of the private individual
we have no objection.'
In the name of national unity
he, General Secretary of the Communist Party,
proposed it should abolish itself
and become an association which wouldn't
'compete with other parties.'
And that's just what happened, on 20th May 44 at the New York Congress
(as a result the Party lost 50% of its members).

(Later, he had a go at the Soviets over the cold war
and was kicked out by his former comrades.
He died at 82, in his bed,
after saying that for a long time
he'd no longer called himself a communist.)

Earl Browder had dreamed that the CPUSA could be in American society
like a fish in water
or perhaps like a submarine, a transparent submarine
with glass sides
that no-one could accuse of anything.
Once the order to dive was given
the submarine disappeared into the depths
and was never found again.

The clocks of the Imperial Palace

The last emperor of the Middle Empire
jealously guarded in the forbidden city
a collection of precious engraved clocks
from Cipango, Bohemia or Veneto.
Did he dream of commanding time?
Or did he already know that his time was up?

Mao's old clothes

When he entered Peking in triumph
Mao owned nothing but a pair of old pyjamas
(and a facecloth).
They say that after that, he always wore patched clothes.
Whenever he had to throw away
a threadbare uniform
he put it on his knees and stroked it
as though a faithful dog about to die.
'I wore it for the Luo Shan conference' he'd say
and he'd run through the service it'd done
since the days of the struggle against Japan.
Then he'd make up his mind: 'I'll not throw it away.
it might still come in handy for repairs.'

(That's the way we should treat the classics.)

Morning snow

After a sleepless night
drinking tea and writing,
Mao went onto his doorstep
and saw the snow covering the earth.
The guard had swept the path.
Mao asked him: 'Why did you do that?'
But the soldier didn't understand.
A little later Mao came back.
Once more the soldier was sweeping to clear the approach.
'Stop!' he said angrily
'The wound had hardly healed…'

(Beneath snow, the world is without contradictions.)

Price setting

Having found out that General Chang Kai Shek
had put a price of a thousand yen
on his head
Mao responded by plastering the walls of the suburbs
and villages
amongst the muddy, loess-filled streets
with posters offering for the capture of his enemy
a reward as great as
one yen.

In a cave in Yenan

While Mao was living in a cave in Yenan,
set up as an office and headquarters,
the approach of the Kuomintang was announced.
His aide-de-camp urged him to leave
but Mao, who had an article to finish, took his time.
When he'd finished, he asked for the cave to be tidied
and that they should leave on the table before disappearing,
a few Marxist works
for the Hu Zhongnan soldiers.

Mao's sleep

When, during the long march
Mao took a rest
to sleep for a while, at the top of a hill
or near a thicket,
there had to be silence.
Even the birds had to be quiet.
And to keep them away his fellow soldiers
waved long poles
with red rags tied to the end.

(Such is the way he behaved towards birds
he, who was also a subtle poet.)

The ball of hard bread

The report arriving at the Palace
announced only success
in the Great Leap forward.
Isolated behind the walls of the Forbidden City
Mao asked himself: 'Is this really the case?'
So to set his mind at rest
in secret, he sent emissaries
to ask a few questions of their families in the countryside.
A little while later, one came back
with a big ball of flour, grass and bark
in his hand.
'This is what our peasants are eating,' said Mao.
And, in tears, he ate the bread very slowly.

(This is a story
from the time of the last Emperors.)

The hall of the yellow crane

During his life, Mao was so loved and admired by the masses
he couldn't set foot out of his palace.
(Even during the Long March
peasants would leave the fields and ditches
to run ahead of the army shouting
'10,000 years of Chairman Mao!'
When in 1952 he went to the hall of the yellow crane
whose view looks over the Yangtse,
his appearance almost caused a riot.
After that, he didn't go into the streets much
but his image was everywhere.
Resisting popularity is hard.
Resisting manipulating it, harder still.
Worshipped like a god,
the Chairman rose into the celestial empire
and the revolutionary left the world of men.

On voluntarism

This is a Chinese fable
(But China, as everyone knows
is a very big country...)
In the region of Szechuan
there lived a peasant
who got up every morning
before the others
to get into the fields
and, to make them grow more quickly,
pulled the heads off his rice plants.
In vain.

As for realism

The young painter went to see the old master
known all over China for his great works.
He found him at home
on his knees in front of a roll of rice paper
working attentively to bring to life with his brush
a pair of blue tits
perched on a bamboo…
For years he'd trained himself
to draw in one flourish
the outlines of birds
and bamboos.
'Master,' he asked
what's the easiest thing in the word
to paint?
'Dragons,' said the master without a thought.
'Dragons?' asked the young painter incredulously.
'Of course. No-one's ever seen one.'

An exploit of the young Kim Il Sung

Even very young
the great leader
supreme helmsman
the well-loved father of the people
and founder of the Juche
astonished his fellows and his teachers
by his practical skill
his theoretical intelligence
and his sense of dialectic.
One day when his teacher asked
what one add one makes
he answered without hesitation, 'One!'
And illustrating his idea with an action
he took a handful of earth in each hand
and made them one
demonstrating
how one and one can make one.
Later he helped expel the Japanese
and the Americans
and set up a State
where the people, the Party and himself
were one
and all other numbers were prohibited.
But he never managed
to bring together
the two parts
of his divided country.

The water's parabola

The waters of the river in spate
which carry everything before them
are stormy, wild and muddy;
all the same, they carry everything before them,
old tyres and the corpses of dead cats,
dead trees, sometimes even breakwaters.
Rain water, baptismal water, washing-up water
water which cleans and purifies never stays pure.

It's when it's crossed the mountains of the night
and has sprung like a new stream
that it's once more transparent and fresh.
When it calms down again,
when the river, the torrent, the streams of history
rest in the glacial cirque.

(But water which stagnates for too long
that too
won't stay pure for long.)

On fallen idols

Those who
last century
brought idols low,
became in their turn, idols,
and in their turn,
were brought low.

(Tell us about it.)

Notes on the International

(now an official song)

Arise, ye prisoners of want
rings out the song at the end of the banquet
(so we could say: the prisoners of hunger
didn't rebel in vain.)
Servile masses, arise, arise!
The generals are reviewing their troops
(their armies billeted over a third of the globe.)
For reason in revolt now thunders
and at last ends the age of cant!
Cosmonaut City celebrates a new mission
but the man in the street (like the boss) consults
astrologers
(and every criticism from below
every idea from the left is forbidden.)
We'll change henceforth the old tradition,
The new order is imposed by guns
and the old world is in the cellar
waiting for the end of the dance...
So comrades, come rally,
And the last fight let us face.
And the last once more will be last.
We'll change henceforth the old tradition,
(On the cleared table he lays you low
and takes you by the throat.)
No more deluded by reaction,
On tyrants only we'll make war!
Stuffed into their overcoats
they wave to the crowd
with a tired hand
on the first of May.
(From the *International* all they've kept is the sound of the brass.)
So comrades, come rally, and the last fight let us face.
The Internationale, unites the human race.
The statues are laid low,
everywhere people are tearing one another to shreds,
we have to start again.

A picture of former times

(From the time of so-called stagnation
when socialism had become
a matter of statistics
when the future was no more than a curve
calculated from present data
and the heart a pond where the waters of the past stagnated.)
It takes place in a factory or on a building site
one first of May or for the anniversary
of the Great October Socialist Revolution.
The workers are gathered amongst their machines
the red flags have been taken out of the cupboards
along with the official banners on which
slogans have been carefully painted by the enterprise
which specialises in the production of calico.

The bosses from the Party, the factory and the union
have taken their place on the platform.
At the end of the meeting the *Internationale* strikes up;
the manager feebly raises his fist and moves his lips
to begin the song whose words he's forgotten
but which the loud-speaker
ghostly but valiant brings back to him:
Arise, ye workers from your slumbers.

About a certain Henri Martin

I can see once more on the platform
my comrade Henri Martin
dutifully seated during a session of the Congress
when his departure from the CC had just been announced.
He's wearing a white shirt and a tie.
On his head, smooth as an apple, his hair is thinning
yet he still has a childlike glint in his eyes.

During the fifties this man was a hero.
A sailor, he was sent to prison for five years
for giving out leaflets calling for peace in Indochina
on a warship.
Before the judge at the Court Martial he declared:
'When you love freedom, you love it for all people.'

Today in certain down-at-heel spots
you can still read on a wall: 'Free Henri Martin!'
And this slogan, which has become a mystery to some,
remains a byword on the long road
to a world without war, without executioners and hate
a world rid of racism and colonialists.

Later, a disciplined man, attached to his Party
and in poor health, he did his work
in the service of the organisation,
without pushing himself forward,
his star gave off no more light than anyone else's.
He was able to content himself with having, for a moment,
given life to a struggle which is enough to give a life meaning.

Henri Martin, a modest man and simple militant
like so many others, wanted to be true to his ideas,
        his comrades, his Party.
But unlike many whose idea of loyalty
led to silence and soon, to giving up thinking,
Henri was one of those who had the simple courage
to think and to defend his ideas.

Ideas get born....

This is how it is with ideas...
The first swallow which opens in the sky
the hostilities of spring
gets gratitude from no-one.
(And soon, those who came after
defy its position and fly ahead.)
Just like the runner who makes a break
and opens the way into sun and pain
then, the main group catch him up and he's absorbed.
That's how it is with ideas.
For a long time, the most revolutionary
run on their own
then they become common property.
Then people forget where they came from
and their triumph is to be forgotten.
Whoever gets up in the morning with a new idea
by evening has to count his white hairs
or put himself in question
and whoever doesn't know that
never enters the race.

The old beast Utopia

– For those of us who claim to believe in scientific socialism
the old hope of Utopia
has kept us blind a long time.
(We knew full well, however,
that what went on there
was no Dream.
But hope was always strongest.
The light of the future flooded the sky
like the Northern Lights.
The entire landscape was transformed...
The factories, the fields, the chimneys,
the muddy holes of the great building sites
and even the mud,
everything took on, thanks to our vision
the look of dawn.)
– We have to have done with Utopia;
send the old bag of bones to the knacker's yard!
– But if you kill the winged beast of the dream
man ceases to march
towards a little more light.
(The dream is necessary;
it simply has to be kept on a leash.)

Father Thu

Clouds, mountains
mountains and clouds
a river below reflects...
At the start of February 1941
Ai Quoc crosses the frontier at checkpoint 108
with his rattan suitcase and his typewriter.
He moves into a cave in Pac-Bo
takes the pseudonym of Father Thu
and begins to organise the Resistance.
Each morning, he goes to the stream.
A rock is his table
(he knows he can rely on the country
because the fight for social liberation
comes through national liberation).
He eats little, but heartily:
corn chowder and bamboo shoots,
receives emissaries
and writes calls to unity and rebellion.
'The life of a revolutionary
is magnificent,' he writes.
In his happy moments
his tracts become poems.
(He has little time for poetry
because all his time is taken up
with poetry.)

Ho Chi Minh's stool

for Nguyen Din Thi

Uncle Ho preferred the gardener's house
to the presidential palace.
For his work, he'd had set up
near the lake, in the palace park,
an open-air office protected simply
from the sun and rain by a straw roof
and near his office, on the ground, he'd put
a little stool.

(He who made the iron tigers of colonialism
tremble.)

He sat there from time to time
to chat and play with the children
who came to see him.

'He is great who keeps the heart of a child,'
Meng Tseu would say.

(You could say too
that by coming down to the level of the smallest
the great
grow greater.)

The ring

for Madeleine Riffaud

The wind above the paddy-fields
is a child driving the black buffalo
of the clouds.
The plane that sparkled in the sun
and brought death to the straw huts
was brought down by the young girl
serving the anti-aircraft corps.
In the photo, the American soldier
(a big blond brute
with the look of a well-fed child)
walks with his hands on his head
in front of a girl fighter, young and slim.
From all around, lines of little men
in black uniforms appear
(like ants, the soldier thought.)
– But ants sometimes get one over on eagles
and this people performed miracles.
The next day,
very skilled hands
cut, from the aluminium body of the Phantom bomber,
a comb and a ring.

Couplets by a messenger about Zapata's horse

Leading the peasants
here comes Emiliano
serious and dreamy guerrilla
astride his white horse.

       'Liberty, Equality'
       those are the aims of the rebels.
       through the mountains and the valleys
       go galloping the radicals.

Looking resolute, proud and disgruntled
he leads into battle his men
who terrorize the soldiers
by shouting 'Land and Freedom.'

       One day, the unworthy Caranza
       (former revolutionary)
       had an idea of how
       to get rid of the unflinching Zapata.

The officer Jésus Guajardo
given the task of capturing him
let the guerrilla know
he was prepared to join the ranks

       and to prove his commitment
       without a regret, without a tear
       he handed over , yes,
       an armed detachment of his men.

Still Zapata was suspicious
as were his commanders
but in the end he agreed
to go to Chinameca.

When Zapata arrived
at the door of the hacienda
the officer said: 'Chief
inside your white horse is waiting for you.'

(In the region everyone knew
Zapata's white horse
he loved it and had given it
one day to a child soldier.

This child had joined them
no-one knows when, in the struggle,
but he disappeared one morning:
went off with the horse.)

Happy to be reunited
Zapata followed the officer
and went into the hacienda
where the soldiers were hidden.

They were stationed on the roofs
their rifles aimed at Zapata.
when he approached the horse
they all fired at once.

That's how Zapata was killed
but amongst the people of the village
no-one identified the face
(you don't kill a Zapata.)

As for the horse, he escaped
over the hills and through the forests
and the soldiers in pursuit
never managed to catch him.

The legend of captain Sandino

for Ernesto Cardenal

In the marshlands where the mangroves twist
along the red sand tracks,
on the edge of the forest greener than a parrot's feathers,
near the enclosure where hens run flapping their wings and
two cocks fight in a splash of fire and
scarlet,
Sandino and his army lay ambushes
for the soldiers of Adolfo Diaz
the dictator in the pay of the Yankees
and behind them they leave feathers and a little blood.
But the pili pili bird sings in the forest
and the people of the little region tell late into the night
tales of Sandino's exploits.
When he'd won and the last of the marines had left
Sandino turned away from the palaces,
from guards of honour
and braided uniforms.
He turned towards the land to make it blossom
towards the too-thin hen, the ear of corn,
towards the child, the woman and the peasant
and he went to work
in one of the co-operatives
he'd founded with his comrades.

But the Yankee eagle
wasn't willing to relax the claws
sunk in the back of the little country.
And the braided uniforms
and the guards
wanted their revenge.
It was their turn to lay a trap:
they invited him to the Palace, to meet the President
and they killed him
with two of his companions.

Years later, however,
in the green and red mountains,
on the slopes of volcanoes,
the boys began to reappear
and in the alleyways of the little region,
on the whitewashed walls,
in the villages an near the shanty towns,
they saw reborn out of the night
the silhouette of the man in the black hat
the comrade
peasant Sandino.

Elegy for Che

I
Che has reappeared in my house
as in the heartlands of Mexico
or Chile or Nicaragua.
His photo is placed on my desk
between the globe
and the old typewriter
made in USA.
Che has moved into my house
with his look of rebellious mischief
to set sparks flying,
his beard is youthful
and he smiles
in spite of fever and asthma
and the contradictions of history.
Che laughs heartily
happy and clear as a morning
when the *maté* begins to boil
in the guerrillas' camp
encircled by mist
Christ fighting with implacable sweetness
Star of the South
utterly earthly angel
of a love without excuse.
He smokes the cigar
and the ash which falls into his tropical beard
in spite of the rain, in spite of the years
sets fire to the mountain.

II
In the faded blue sky of the map
          South America
has the tortured body of a man who's been hung
and from the open wounds left by its executioners
fall children of light.
Che is a child fallen to earth
and – after walking

the trails of human suffering
       along the back of the crippled continent –
the footloose child
gathered together his doctor's things
and took up arms.

III
In the Sierra Maestra
at the time of the revolutionary war
(this is taken from the Golden Legend of the Saints
who sometimes bled for the Revolution)
harassed, the guerrillas route march across the mountains
Che
       hampered by asthma
                     says to Fidel:
'Leave me, I'm holding you back,'
but Fidel refuses to hear.

IV
'Beauty is not angry,'
you said
'with the Revolution.'

V
Che,
comrade minister
you drive a tractor and you play
you hold in your hand the machete
of the sugar cane fighters
guerrillas of production
but even Cuban earth
so light
sticks to your feet
and the sky is heavy.
'The socialist economy,'
you say
without the spirit of communism
doesn't interest me.'
The way hardly opened up
you have to make a new start.

VI
Che
you never knew
the shame of growing old
of putting on weight
of adjusting to
little rewards
and great sadness.
You never knew
the ashen taste
of resignation.

VII
Betrayed by those
you were fighting for
you got lost
in the cold and the green,
on the paths of an austere country,
but the wrong turns
the military disaster
isolation and defeat
in the earthy night
and in the dark heart of the people
as if by magic
were transformed
into a source of light.

VIII
Che
you have reappeared in my house
and on the shelves of supermarkets
on shop displays
on CD inserts
printed on T-shirts
or on the chrome of cigarette lighters
a new image to buy and sell,
super-consumer prize
in the great beauty contest
of martyrs and rebels.
Capitalism gobbles up

all rebellions
and lives off
the very source
of its destruction.
Che
you are the incurable dream
of a world without dreams
and without revolutions
a dream which wakes you up in the middle of the night.

IX
Comandante Che
this evening
            sitting at my typewriter
            a cigar in my mouth
            in the middle of green plants
I ask myself who said:
'Revolution is a bicycle;
if you stop pedalling
            you fall off.'

May-June '68

(Song without nostalgia)

In May, sweet May, sleeping France was roused
  in the streets, young people played knuckle bones
    and beneath their hands the paving stones came to life!

The trees in the streets throw dog collars into the gutters!

No more bosses! no more platforms! friendliness all round!
  in verbal violence and amongst the tear-gas
    we rediscover the word brotherhood!

Youth is an uncapped geyser of anger!

In May, sweet May, everything at last seems possible.
  'Under the pavement, the beach!' In the towns, a spring
    bursts into flower. 'Be realistic, ask for the impossible!'

Let's blow up the paper dam of the everyday so the great
wave of the dream can spread everywhere!

On factories and schools the red flag waves
  we set up committees, assemblies where I hold the floor.
    You, you learn *The Inter...* The world is shifting.

The crowd is like a clenched fist around the neck
of the avenues, the squares and the bridges!
At the Place Nationale, the people are in the streets!

Both of us stammer the vocabulary of revolution.
  We imitate the workers and their occupations
    and without claiming to, we practise self-management.

In our hearts is a conspiracy of tulips!

In Paris, in Prague, in Rome, Tokyo or San Francisco
  love has decreed the crowning of birds
    and peaceful people will have flowers for flags.

They can always shoot the blackbird's song at point blank range,
we don't muzzle the clouds!

(Charlety...' the darlings are counter-revolutionary!'
        And these 'revolutionaries' are anti-communist!'
        At the first kiss, the revolution was aborted.

Tanks, disarray and sunflowers...) Lenin, wake up, they've
gone mad!

Spring is under lock and key. In the water, the hope of renewal.
        Utopia remains, the insolence of ideals
                and the rejection of the indefatigable 'trip, work, kip'.

Cuba – Festival of youth

In Cuba
            the youth of the world
meets Revolution in the street
the people are all smiles.
Standing on the terrace
I wait for the dances to end...
Tonight the island could float away
and we would establish a continent
of free and beautiful
                        men and women

But our love binds us to the earth

(This is an ancient memory...)

Dialogue on self-government

for Volker Braun

Outside, in the orchard under the window
the apple trees are hung with green fruit,
– two heedless young girls
                          play on the swings –
some, left to themselves,
have fallen to the ground
and are already rotting.
– They weren't ready, it seems
                          for self-government.
– No doubt,
but if you wait too long, ripeness is squandered.

The opening

When they opened the door
and then the windows
the house collapsed.
Who's to blame?
The architect?
The building materials?
The workers?
Or whoever opened the windows?

The burial of Henri Lefebvre

In the graveyard at the foot of the Pyrenees the red roses
     sit upright on their stalks
Above us, an unpredictable sky holds back –
       for how long – from sending us scurrying beneath
       torrents of water.
The lorries which pass by on the road below keep the dead
      awake.
As soon as the sun reappears between two showers the hornets come back.
A police helicopter flies high above
      the sparse gathering.
The State never leaves us alone, moribund, ubiquitous.
Glass vases and artificial flowers sit on the
      headstones
The everyday keeps going
(and ceaselessly the obscure voice of the dead, amongst the humans
      dominated by their mysteries,
comes to take possession of the minds of the living
which rely on abstract forces.)
The occasion has brought together the priest, the mayor, the daughters,
      the lovers, architects, a successful town planner, a
      communist psychoanalyst,
       an old reactionary sociologist, a theorist of Italian self
       government,
       a more or less reformed terrorist, new and old friends,
       a scattered handful of grain…
With a speech which takes its sad revenge on the living likeness
(of hopelessness, we will be spared nothing.)
Ah, the misfortune of being silent in the hands of your friends…
Many loved him and all betrayed him.
And then, when all's said and done, it's the most reliable of his works…
(Is there a true master who doesn't give rise to his own betrayers?)
He didn't build systems but was a happy destroyer
an indefatigable interrogator
who by having the courage to think made his listeners
      more intelligent,
a vigorous walker in the mountains
and on the human routes of the crucified sun.

Having seen before others
how those who wanted to eliminate
the old system of exploitation
recreated in their turn domination and alienation
he never gave up looking for new paths
for the revolution.
In his attic full of light from the Pyrenees
or in the common room with a glass of wine,
the philosopher kept open house.
But in the end visitors became rarer.
Sitting in his armchair, by the fire, in the great
            frozen house
a blanket over his stiff legs,
unable to walk,
he remained till the end attentive to life's movement
to what was happening world-wide;
like a young man ready to take the road
to a better future.
After the burial, we came home on foot.
Groups of young people had gathered
into a little, improvised university.
In the big house, the hearth is growing cold,
a little more wood is needed on the fire.
Before leaving, you picked a four-leafed clover
            in Catherine's garden.
Hope and a taste for happiness have a hard time.

'When the struggle flourishes, winter goes on strike'

(read on a wall, December 1995)

Those of us who have May in our hearts
are brought low by the cold of November.
The snow shook his eiderdown at the window
and powdered our heads
as for Paris's sun, usually so waggish,
he'd taken on the sad look of days of bad weather
(as if he shared our determination.
But let's forget the sky
which doesn't have much to do
       with what we're talking about).
That year in towns across France
people never seen on the telly
were headline news.
We saw those who keep things going
and are, today as in the past,
last in the dinner queue,
       lording it.
The working class they said had disappeared
       came back to life.
And the buried class struggle
rose from the tomb
and walked its happy ghost
       across squares and down avenues.
We saw railway workers marching
       red torches in their hands
(because Lucifer and Prometheus are still among us)
and electricians beat on oil drums
(because African gods too were summoned.)
The barbarians who camp in the city
have set winter ablaze.
And at the braziers they lit
they've been able to warm themselves
because these barbarians
       are the really civilised ones.

Fighting for social security,
they were fighting for civilization
because no society is worth the name
if it allows
some of its people to die on the pavement.
'United we stand!'
'United we stand!' was the slogan of those days.
It doesn't seem to say much
but – for many – it said a great deal
because in the city
where isolation reigns
to come together
       this is
       the question of questions
the end
and the means.
If the general strike is not only a carnival
there is no general strike without celebration.
Because the strike breaks the monotonous cycle of dead time.
It isn't revolution of course
but a foretaste
because revolution is perhaps merely
the self-organisation of the masses
the people at last grown up.
We hold general assemblies
and we learn to stammer democracy
and as everyone's voice can be heard
everyone is responsible for what he says.
Those who yesterday walked past one another
stuffed into their watertight divers' suits
talk to one another, use first names and walk side by side.
Even private cars
usually the cockpits for solitary creatures
turn into collective transport.
Everyone comes out of their shell and life pulls itself together.
It won't last long of course....
We'll have to start again.
And then once more.
Even tomorrow.
We'll have to break the ice-floe

over and again
because life in society is like water which freezes.
But
this year
the November strikers
declared spring just as winter was setting in.

THE WORLD'S SONG

Man's torment

for Aragon

Man often lives on just fresh air
False hope and real weary care

If he believes in god, god tells lies
Within him his world shrinks in size

Time for him is vain Novenas
We haven't got a bean between us

Earth is a mere hellish garden
Our hearts against each other harden

That man passing in the street
Walks upon a stranger's feet

To himself man is a stranger
In every other he spies danger

Some chase their shadows like mad
Dogs through the ruins of what they had

They yelp and rip themselves apart
Tear the love from their own hearts

Many in these troubled times
Take the road that leads to crime

We see them walking in our crowd
But they lurk behind a shroud

Wishing to take off for the stars
They fall asleep like drunks in bars

By dreaming so much what life might give
You lose the very will to live

Living on dreams is a risky game
Without a dream life has no name

Not much though would do the trick
A happy song renews life's quick

Or to know the future's ours
A little, comforts present hours

Not to live in ourselves curled
To bring to life a human world.

At the 'Sylvia Villa'

In Barbusse's garden
                    the poplars whisper,
in the 'Sylvia Villa'
                    survives the lively memory
of a history
            of a united people.
The walls of the house
                    are hung with red flags
                    – it's like the inside of a heart –
Flags of hope at half mast
great Cholet handkerchiefs stained with blood
waved at the window of a smoke-blackened train
on the platform of the past
like a 'Farewell'…
like a 'Hello'
                    for the living.
Outside and under the June sky
                        the war is already far away.
Peace is woven from a billion blades of grass
a charming brass band with shining
instruments
            beats the ceremony's time
like a happy dog
wagging its tail.
The old-timers, the flag bearers
wait patiently for the speeches to end
a cock-a-doodle-do sparks up in the village
the cry of joy of a French cock
old soldier
valiant defender of the peace of farmyards
courting a hen
                    and crowing his love.
In Barbusse's garden
                    rose bushes flourish
And in the shade of a hedge
                    a delicate honeysuckle
                    entwines itself

like an ear
like a kiss.
Near the vegetable garden
stands a round table
– so knights can take a rest –
a stone table
with a beard of lichen
which welcomes us, splendidly
for our aperitif.
Pierre,
Lubomir
and me
the women and the friends.

A little further on near the bushes
Barbusse keeps vigil
his chest narrow
his eyes bright
and fine as paper
his smile
straight as a blade
Statues (is it coincidence?)
can't talk.
All the same I can imagine him asking us:
'Tell me
my young friends,
what have you done with the years
with our ideas
with our hopes
with our loves?...'

We'll pick our words with care
We'll be a bit embarrassed
Then, one of us
(Lubomir,
Pierre,
or me? Who knows?)
at last will decide to speak:
'You know
nothing is ever written.

In truth
it didn't happen
as we'd expected.
Often we thought
we'd taken hold of it
the beauty,
the promise
And so many times it escaped us
leaving on our lips
a little blood mixed with ash…
Sometimes, we find it hard
to remember what it looks like
like a woman we dream we're in love with
forgotten on waking
and desperately searched for…'

Perhaps

he wouldn't understand
('certainly', he'd think,
'poets will never be cured
of their obscurity…')

Perhaps, on the contrary.
we would see his stone bust
nod in approval
and say to us:
'That's good, my dears
carry on…'

The rose laurels of democracy

for Yannis Ritsos

Here's what I brought back from Athens:
in the plane which banks on its wing
a frieze of geometric shapes
                sky blue on beige
(of the kind which must have graced
the clothes of the ancient Greeks)
the sea
and the whole landscape
                seen from the window
a view of the airport
the action of the policeman searching my bags
looking for suspect books
a hotel lift
and a lift attendant
who gives me the icy eyeball
(and this image:
democracy has just revived
but
   as at the victory of Samothrace
something's missing)
In the streets there's a sense of joy with time on its hands
The kiosks and the cafes are full
The banks' doors are smoked glass
(they could come from anywhere)
and nearby, on the pavements
the children
         collectors of miracles
               sell sponges
plucked from the bottom of the sea.
It's hot…
At the crossroads centaurs wear uniforms
Little groups of protesters,
flags in their hands,
             pass one another on the squares.
In a stadium (above the town)
a hundred thousand young people

sing Ritsos and Theodorakis
in unison.
But everyone senses
                poetry is fragile
The Acropolis is a pile of stones.
Here, the presence of man
                        although here for millennia
has hardly made an impression
                        on the sky.
In the evening, I find myself on the terrace
of a low grade restaurant
in Piraeus
drinking Retsina beneath a trellis of virgin vines
with a young man
sporting a partisan's moustache
He's a plumber and just out of prison
he's serene
he knows what he wants
and while he speaks he counts his rosary

From Athens
                I brought back a rosary
                a simple rosary
                made of red plastic beads
                my only jewellery
                I take it everywhere
                on my wrist
                sometimes I lose it
                I always find it again.
I held it between my fingers in the car taking me
to the airport
and in my memory
the rose laurels
                covered in dust in the middle of the road
                        are still flowers.

Letter to Chilean friends

for Sergio Ortega

Chile
    came in through the window
    with a rough woollen scarf around her neck
    with a face of brass, luminous and profound
    with clay hands
Chile
     came into our life
            unexpectedly, almost
                    like a Spring day
Her look
        was well-known – that of a child saying:
          'Now I'm wearing
        long trousers!'
        and in her hand she held
        the bluish joy of a glass of milk.
One day, Chile
        came into our house
        wearing pauper's clothes
      – the one
      without knowing it
            we'd always been waiting for –
She sat at the table
            broke the bread
            of Dignity
and said to us: 'Eat
            this belongs to us.'
One day, Chile came into our life
and since
        she's never left.
So we've turned
        towards the other side of the globe
and for you
        my friends from the other hemisphere
we have relearned
        our geography

We ran our hands over the
  the long flower in your button hole
  which your Cordillera
              is to the planet
we gazed intently at
      your snow-covered vines
      your towns, your miners
we dreamed of writing
love poems for you
          shining unpolished silver
like the phases of the moon
sealed in bottles and thrown into the sea
so the waves could wash them up
in Valparaiso.
Or, to put it another way:
        your slim homeland
        had become so important to us
        strange and so distant
she seemed near at hand
        She resembled
                our horizon
(We too believed in
the peaceable power of volcanoes.)

Until the early telegraphic morning of the crime
        when we found out
        – in anger and powerlessness –
        that a boot was crushing
        the sturdy red flower
        of Araucania
And so it was
        as if your land
                deep as a wound
        and as long as exile
                had plunged into southern night.

One day, Chile came into our homes
and we took over
        the scattered-papers poet's roses
        the salt kisses laid down by the sea
        the patience of saltpetre

the soaked southern forests
the lunar northern sun, your drifting mists
your songs and your flags.

All these years
of this dark history of solidarity
while streams made their way beneath the ground
we lived them together.

Today,
it's winter in Paris
summer in Santiago
the streets once more have begun to sing
and from the windows
butterflies make their escape.

The ballad of Bobby Sands

Just after two in the morning
his heart stopped
then suddenly there was great silence
the soldiers of the British empire
went to earth
tight against one another
in their iron coffins,
Big Ben kept quiet
St George withdrew in shame.
In Westminster in the common rooms
even the armchairs bent their backs
the Irish night stood upright
behind a mummy named Thatcher;
for her it's always five o'clock
and she's drinking tea with biscuits
dunked in blood.
Floating on the tea the blind eyes of Bobby Sands
are as bad as it gets.
They chew strips of blackened flesh
in silence with their pinkies raised.
The International of the cowards
is invited for tea
but bones are hard to swallow.

In the streets, the Belfast children
wear their hair green
on days of anger
hair of wild grass which conquers the hills
above the sea
and in their hands
like grenades
they hold tight
clods of their earth.

Mandela for life

(lullaby to prevent falling asleep)

I
Mandela
          let the noises die down
Mandela
          let's listen to the night.
To the stars
          the murmurs fly
and the wind
          brings them towards you.

We sing so that the dawn
of a more human life
might set violence aside
and suffering
          be transformed into seed.
Mandela, let the noises die down,
let the night bring us your look.

II
Mandela
          let walls be swept away
Mandela
          let the night bring us together.
The sowing
          has made the earth fecund
in secret
          our crops are growing to fullness.
Listen how the world
breathes close to your heart.
It's getting ready to smile
just like a sleeping child
          in a dream.
Mandela, let walls be swept away
let the night bring us close to you.

III
Mandela
       let our hands welcome you
       Mandela
       let this day be yours.
We sing
       the lullaby of a world
which tomorrow
       will wake up in peace.

No night is so dark
nor death so powerful
nor these chains so strong
that they can stop us
that they can hold us back

Mandela, let our hands welcome you,
Mandela, let this day be yours.

Mandela
       let the noises die down
Mandela
Mandela for life.

(in collaboration with Sergio Ortega who wrote the music for this lullaby)

Moscow

for Yevgeny Yevtushenko

Yesterday I went to Red Square

In the dark blue night the paving stones shone
like the scales of a chocolate fish
wrapped in silver paper.
A scarlet star
              like a candle
sitting on the Kremlin
and 'Basil the Blessed'
the colour of barley sugar
– the architects (on the orders of the Tsar)
had their eyes gouged out –
                    dreaming of the sky
            waiting no doubt
                    for a coming take-off.
Close by
        – you can hardly believe it –
                    sleeps Lenin.
From the four corners of the planet
young people who don't know one another
            have arranged to meet
here.

Lighter than sponge divers
they plunge into the night
and gather smiles, names, memories…

A little wind of liberty blows
Red Square has put up its sails
and
          (everyone can see)
when you stand up
            on the fish's body
    beneath your feet, you feel – distinctly –
            that our earth
                is round!

Nostalgia for Leningrad

I
Pushkin Square, a young girl
seventeen, very blonde
sitting in her white dress, delicately
on the plinth of a statue
her arms round her knees and her head tilted
as she dreams
(perhaps she's a pupil of Marius Petitpas's Kirov ballet).

II
At the entrance to the Hermitage
you have to put on impressive imitation felt grey footwear
to protect the floors

Where did the painters from the twenties go?

The past is worthy of respect
but the future too.

III
Beneath the bridges of the Neva seen in reflection
a turbulent water rushes incessantly
(somewhere up stream a giant samovar
is hidden.)
Enthroned in their chairs, the canteen ladies
look like huge paper puppets
protecting the tea-pots.
(Don't trust the silence.
A strange thaw is brewing here…)

IV
Along the quay, the cruiser Aurora
emerges from the mist.
Her cannons have long been silent.
Who will keep the memory
of the beauty of the first red flags
put up on the factories and palaces?

And what cruiser from the high seas
used to black expanses
where all moves and blends
will fire the salvo of a new hope?

Berlin '89

In the middle of Berlin, near the Town Hall
a cockstride from the former Reichstag,
just after the fall of the Wall,
on the plinth of the monument to Marx and Engels
(where you see Marx sitting, looking profound, solid and sombre
and Engels, standing
faithfully behind)
an anonymous hand has written these words:
'We'll do better next time.'

To the students of Tiananmen Square

for Wang Meng

Tiananmen or: The Square of Celestial Peace
'Bad translation'
(so a scholarly friend tells me)
...due no doubt to the old habit
of always romanticizing the Orient.
The translation should be 'entrance' not 'square'
(where foreigners
before coming into the Forbidden City
were required to bow in the reverential kowtow)
And furthermore not 'Celestial Peace'
but 'Pacification' (from above)
– But no difficulty in translation can justify the blood
nor the bullet at point blank range
in the starred head of the revolution –
(Empires always hatch rotten eggs)
Between the Peking students and ourselves
there are no problems of translation
The same scintillating words circulate
the kite-words of freedom
and the notes of a song of youth:
The Internationale.

Free enterprise

On Wenceslas Square
close by the white building where the democratic Forum
has just set itself up
a young, blond, smiling man
(no doubt a brilliant student
from an economics course)
has set up a new stall
with a wooden sign on which he has painted
in big, well-formed letters
his advertising slogan:
'Jan Janacek
first free-market shoe-shine boy
of the East.'

Things seen in Budapest

In Varosliget Park
they've set up temporarily deck chairs
and camping tables
so vendors can offer tourists relics of communism:
insignia of the Communist Youth
belt buckles from the Red Army
party cards and military caps.
They're also selling little, round, metal boxes
like boxes of catechu
on which is written (in Hungarian and German)
'The final breath of communism'
(here capitalism is getting business going again
by selling wind).
On a cornice of a baroque castle
a real cinematic setting
where all the styles of the country's history are on display
a stone marquis
holds the hand of a shepherdess.
The visitors pay hardly any attention
to this decorative and outdated couple
who hold aloft the pastoral idyll
and understanding between classes
but when no-one's watching the little marquis lifts his foot
puffs up his chest and skips a minuet
because the good times are returning.
Like yesterday however old pot-bellied inhabitants of Budapest
go on with their game of chess
sink in the warm waters of the bath of Szechenyi Furdo.
Nothing seems to have changed
but in the dark water of these Austro-Hungarian pools
worrying eddies appear.
The old nationalist and anti-semitic Hungary
returns to the surface.
All the same, outside in the sun,
parked near the trees along the pavement
a pair of lovers kiss
in a little blue car.

In Bucharest a sentry sleeps

Bucharest April 1990

This is the country of the sleeping soldiers.
An invisible girl sitting on their knees
caresses their bewildered faces
beyond the window on which dust has long gathered
horses harnessed in pain collapse.
Cap on their heads, their mouths agape
a lazy rifle leaning against the chair.
Will Sleeping Beauty wake them from their dream of blood
with a kiss?
On the dark corner of the street burn yellow candles
for the Christmas dead, the angels of December.
A butchered guilty tulip in a glass
wonders who stole her colours.
The castles of Happiness are never done adding up
          their ruins.
The soldiers, who fell asleep during their guard duty,
visit countries long dreamed of in vain
and their heads lean against unsteady walls
from behind bearded witches who
offer you an apple and eat your ear
In the morning float unharnessed horses.
Freedom is an old nag with steaming flanks
ridden by a whore.
The laws of gravity have started showing off.
The empty universe wears a feathered hat
a transient rainbow to rest her buttocks on.
The straight lines of perspective
have let the horizon fall
which without them is no longer anything at all.
(Our heraldry no longer speaks.)
The world is a wonky picture which has lost its frame
it goes into the street and finds itself handsome.
In the midst of the flakes, the trees in Spring
the Future has been sacked
and the present is this arrested snow…
The sleeping soldier knows nothing of the route
but he imagines it will be his

Muddy Sofia

On a little snow-covered square
women have hung on the branches
embroidered doilies
like a curtain of frost
in a fairy tale.
Since the fall of the communists
the picture of the claimant to the throne
has begun to be seen on walls
but no-one seems to notice.

Dimitrov's mausoleum
has been turned into a urinal.
The town is sinking into cold and mud.

I go with Blaga to the bus stop,
she takes my arm
and we head into the night
along narrow paths
cleared in the snow by the locals.
Near the square where children were playing during the day
the great poet who gave her voice to the opposition
stops and asks me:
'Is the only future left for all of us
to become shopkeepers?'

At the airport
a cleaning woman is pushing her floor cloth in front of her
as she drags her feet.

Everywhere there is so much to clean away.

Four postcards from ex-Yugoslavia

*

A road by the sea on the Dalmatian coast
nature denuded
the water very pure
people swim around the boat
among the islands
shishkebab and slivovitz.
No-one asks
your grandfather's name.
This place is not far
from the borders of paradise.

*

On the bend
a swift Mercedes
cuts up a lorry.

Everyone walks
with a bank-note stuck their forehead.

'Here,' a friend says, 'war
is just a particular way
of privatising the economy.'

*

A high road
between Bosnia
Serbia and Croatia.
Ruins.
All the houses bombarded.
Cannons firing from one side and another.
The very trees
bare and shredded
(War, painted by douanier Rousseau).
From time to time
a UN control post
a Muslim cemetery

a Christian cemetery.
(The cemeteries on the hills
are bloated.)
And all the way in the dark
the lights
of shops and night bars.

No longer any question of self-government.
Internationalism was a dream
What remains is the real nightmare
of nationalism.
A great dream, when you let it fail
can lead to much bloodshed.

*

In the field of sparse grass
in the middle of the rocks
beneath a steel-blue sky
a peasant has written
with big stones
the name of Tito.

Song of the Russian doll

(craftsman critique of the traditional)

In the window of *Beriozka*
the Russian doll holds court
on the gift counter.

You open the first model
of a sleeping apparatchik

Inside hides the model
of a businessman, a real bandit.

Divide it, you'll find
inside a priest or a gangster

And each time the wretched toy
is a little smaller.

Will history be so written
that in order to read the future
all we have to do is split its great head?

The trial of Pol Pot

The grey-haired man is sitting on a simple chair
judged by his fellows who find him now
       too burdensome
beneath the awning of a straw hut somewhere in the Cambodian
       countryside
on the edge of a forest with emerald green foliage.
The man is affable and smiling, with a look of great
       gentleness,
a Khmer scarf round his neck,
like an elegant slip-knot.
(In the forest with the emerald green foliage
are trees whose roots feed on blood.)
A few poor peasants are there.
(They seem marginally interested in the event.)
they add their twopenneth to the accusations
(but on their faces is no trace of hatred
nor even anger)
(on the monuments hidden by the wild vegetation
Buddha too looks indifferent
but the peasants are thinner.)
This very gentle man
is accused of having massacred his people.
'We lacked experience,' he says,
to excuse his crimes.
Son of a poor peasant, he was brought up in a pagoda
and has retained the taste for purity learned there.
At the start of the underground movement he lived amongst
       a tribe
and was full of enthusiasm for its egalitarian and frugal
       way of life.
With his comrades, he wanted to purify the country
       of western corruption
and to return to the ancient communism of the peasants.
To permit the resurrection and redemption of their
       people
the Khmers Rouge didn't hesitate to massacre them,

finally, isolated and beaten, they took refuge in the forest
and the forest devoured them.
The pure nationalists made a pact with the devil.
In order to buy weapons,
they went into emerald mining
on behalf of the West.
Little by little, their ranks thinned out...
(Yeng Sari, the faithful companion
defected taking 4,000 men with him.)
Son Sen, the good comrade, also betrayed the cause.
His family had to be massacred.
Today, Pol Pot is sitting beneath the awning of a straw hut,
ready to pardon.
He who sent hundreds of thousands of men and women to
their deaths
won't be condemned to death
but to live, without any role.
Pol Pot, so gentle and tired, smiles.
He knows he'll escape
justice when he's found guilty.

The Fifth International

I
During the night
            we crossed
The Channel
(by the Shuttle,
            no waves
            no stars
            no siren)

We crossed
quietly
            through the night's
      channel
and landed
in the nick of time in a City bar
at breakfast time
– two fried eggs
a skinny sausage
a lemon tea
and a Portuguese waitress –
and coiled in the pit of our stomachs,
the hypnogogic snake of sleep
and a mission: a meeting
in Westminster Hall
with Trotskyists
several hundred dangerous syndicalists
from England, Germany, Spain
Russia and France
dockers from Liverpool
dockers' wives
and honourable
although in the minority and outside convention
Members of Parliament
all united
against the EU of bankers
and for the International.

II
This is an old idea,
and no longer in fashion
All the same
the nineteenth century marches on our heels.
London is a golden cuff-link
huge and brash
sticking out of a crumpled smoking jacket.
Everywhere in the streets
– as in all streets
in very modern and democratic
capitalist capitals –
men and women are sleeping under cardboard.
Fallen
from the pockets of smoking jackets on the tarmac of towns
like pinches of tobacco,
as worthless
as dandruff
you brush off your shoulders.

III
Big Ben
is the umbrella pointing towards the sky
of the ghost of a colonel from the Indian army
who can't retreat.

His walrus moustache
is lying on a flea market stall
in Petticoat Lane
gathering dust.

But the colonel still dreams
of charging, his sabre drawn,
for the glory of Empire
and Civilisation...

While the waiter
in the Indian restaurant
serves lamb curry
Soho fashion.

IV
In the standard bed and breakfast room
(rented by a Pole on his uppers)
twin beds set a distance between us
like a channel of silence in the dark.
Are we nothing more on earth
than straws carried on the tide?
But tonight the idea
– still in it's elementary state –
of a new International
building new bridges
between the workers of the whole world
sketches on the sombre water of sleep
moired and phosphorescent reflections
like a dream about to be realised…

V
Before leaving London
we went to see Marx again
out of the fray on his Highgate hill
in the middle of red roots and broken tombs
(It costs a pound
to visit the old lion
crouched in his cage of death;
unless you're one of the family
– maybe we'll say that next time –)
'How can you,'
the tough-minded will ask,
'as Marxists,
practice the worship of the dead?'
All religions have their rituals, even that
which aims to put men in the place of gods.
That's why, strange as it seems,
we too
we believe
          in spirits
                    and in the life
                              (eternal or almost)
of the best ideas…
This Sunday morning in the cemetery

we experienced something
like a presence
in the fleeting appearance
          of a squirrel with a grey tail,
and the chance encounter
of a pair of lovers
a theatre producer and his wife
(wearing a cap with a pacifist badge)
a Japanese guy and us,
all gathered
in front of the headstone on which is written:
'Workers of all countries unite'
and also:
'Philosophers have only
interpreted the world,
the point is to change it.'

Prayer for western civilization

'Everyone must understand, this is about a stand-off between civilization and barbarism.' (Jacques Chirac)

We are civilized, because our missiles are
        the fastest
We are civilized because our Apache helicopters
        are without rival in the market
We are civilized because we have law and
        television on our side
We are civilized because we know only force
        the price of oil and the control of uranium
We are civilized because we decide who
        are the good and the bad, who are
        the dictators and the democrats,
We are civilized because we have the power to decide
        who has or hasn't the right to be a refugee
We are civilized because we prosecute humanitarian
        wars
And when inadvertently we kill a few hundred civilians
        by bombarding a shelter, a convoy of lorries
        or a residential area
It's enough for us to say these are unfortunately
        collateral costs hard to avoid in time of war
and we can go on making peaceful war.
We are the civilized and we are going to win.
We've already defeated the Picts who painted themselves
        blue
and the plains warriors who had only arrows
and charged down hills bareback on their horses.
All these savages from America, Africa and Asia who
        killed one another, we brought together
by slaughtering them.
We are the strongest.
We will soon re-enter Rome, and pass in our
        immaculate chariots under the triumphal arches
and women from distant lands brought as a tribute
        will spread rose petals beneath our feet…

All the same, sometimes in the evening, we wonder,
anxiously
how much longer this is going to last?
In fact,
more and more often, in the four corners of the empire, we
        have to intervene.
And the battle is unequal because the barbarians are
numerous,
        more and more numerous,
and life for those people
is cheaper
than for us, the civilized,
because us, we don't like to die..
So we wonder:
How long
how much longer
can it go on?...
How much longer will the rest of humanity
be able to put up with us?

NY.NY. 9.11

A plane in the sky, which banks on its wing with the slowness
        of a shark
in the middle of the blue skies of the telly screen.
Everybody on Earth, as usual, had their eyes fixed on
Olympus:
a restaurant with a view over the Hudson,
a swimming-pool full of clouds
        on the top floor
the white warriors of the Stock Exchange are seated around
        their oval table.
(They throw their missiles
 like paper aeroplanes onto the world
not thinking, that somebody could do the same to them)
at that height, crystals form in the heart.

High pressure over New York
('It's a good day to die'
says the old sachem
on the television.)

When people saw
        (at the same instant all around the Earth)
                the first plane smash into the tower
they at first thought it was an accident.
The net of neurons of the radar screens and towers
        must have broken down.
Then the other plane arrived.
And the towers of the World Trade Centre
were brought to their knees
but it was too late to pray
and Manhattan disappeared in a cloud of smoke
like an octopus which hides in its cloud of ink.
(That,
every one of us saw.)
By crashing into the towers

the planes brought to the ground the totems
the white warriors had set up at the tip of the island
and that day
(a beautiful day of blue skies over the town)
death was invited to the table.

Return to sender
the desert storm has retraced its steps
the winds blow right round the Earth
and whoever sows the wind reaps the whirlwind.
The empire is at war
the masters of the world have set free from their box
the demons under their command which slept in the dark.

Every day, hordes of bats gather at the summit of the towers
they take their flight and spread in swarms to the four corners
          of the world.

To liberate yourselves, realize your fantasies! repeats the
psychoanalyst
          of 5th Avenue.
For years the United States of America has sent us their televised
                                                  nightmares
they are the first producers of horror films in the world
and now the bad dreams of their film merchants
are incarnated and return to them full in the face.
(You shouldn't play with dreams.)
In the panic which followed, we saw a dazed woman
who wandered in the street covered from head to foot by a veil
          of yellow dust
similar to the veiled women elsewhere
one among millions of others
a victim of war.

In the middle of the avenues of shattered asphalt
close to the barriers hastily put up by the fire-fighters
silent ghosts passed
whose invisible image was not imprinted on the screen
(they simply made something like a trembling of heat in the air)
the dead of Vietnam, the dead of Chile, the dead of Indonesia,

the dead of Panama, the dead of Ruanda,
Palestinians caught in the trap of the 'final solution',
the dead of Yugoslavia
the children of Iraq
for whom the television
does not bestir itself.

They are all there, filing past unhurriedly
as in one of those films where the clocks stop
when the extra-terrestrials descend on the Earth
and they pass among the ruins
indifferent to the drama.

But business picks up again
newspapers dated 11 September sell for as much as 200 dollars
in the hours which follow, an internet site opens
to offer the rubble of the two towers for huge prices
and, thanks to the attacks,
the military budget of the United States
beats all records
at last it'll be possible to have recourse to nuclear arms
at last it'll be possible to embark on new wars
let business thrive!

In the parks, the New Yorkers form into circles
like Indians around their fires
they take one another by the hand and pray.
Are they going to hear the murmur of the dead
of the whole Earth?

(If they want the words of their prayer to reach the ears
of an all-powerful humanity
they will need to enlarge the circle
and allow the other people of the Earth
the barefoot
the ragged
the under-developed
to take them by the hand
to teach them new songs.)

Report on the state of the world

(10 March 2002, morning)

This morning, on waking, I saw heading north a triangular flight
        of migrating birds. My neighbour told me they
        were cranes.
The American army hasn't caught Bin Laden yet
        nor Mullah Omar gone to ride his moped
        in the Afghan mountains.
The lilac is ready to flower, at the end of its branches
        great pale green buds have formed which want only
        to burst open.
Are we going to put up much longer with them crippling the world
        before our very eyes
that its hands are tied behind its back and its skull cracked
        with a rock, like in a Jebel during the
        Franco-Algerian war?
The first dandelions are exploding silently into life in the grass
        you just have to turn your head to come across
        new little suns.
The Bush administration – which preaches liberalism and the end
        of tariff barriers for the entire planet, has decided
        to increase by 30% taxes on the import of steel
        to the USA.
My son has got up, he pulls on his back-pack and gets ready to go out
        to find himself an apprenticeship.
In the areas of the Arab towns occupied by the Israeli army
        the Tsahal soldiers have branded
        the Palestinians with a number on the forearm.
Are we going to put up much longer with Israeli helicopters
        bombarding private cars in the streets,
        killing men, women and children in cold blood?
This morning, I came across a pair of partridges by the side of the road
        waddling along peacefully in a ploughed field.
To help the war on terror, the American military budget
        has been increased by 350 million dollars.
Le Monde announces in its most recent edition that the French army
        is putting together a manual for urban warfare.

(This news causes hardly a stir in the media.)
The empire is threatening because it's threatened.
(The United States is the most
        indebted country in the world. They
        live on the backs of others and that's why they have to
        dominate the planet. From their weakness they
        draw their strength.
        But their strength is the cause of their weakness.)
Today, I poured a glass of wine from
        the new year's vat,
Patricia has got up for breakfast,
Life on Earth has no need of masters.

POEMS FOR A NEW DAWN

Hope's counter-melody

There was a time not long ago
When we knew the future by heart

But this time is now forgotten
And the spring dresses in mourning

Cold is spreading which seems obvious
Clear and which resounds like a conquering winter

In the sky the stars, weary of shining
No longer light our night on earth

Who can flourish in the land of ice?
The dawn is hung on a butcher's hook

It has known its harvest of interdictions
Sad forest with a defeated look

Frenzied water of dams that break
We have seen the world recovered

A few houses torn apart by the flood
And roots rotting in bright sunlight

We have seen great winds which turned
The weathercocks clinging to the roofs

On the horizon, water held sway unchallenged
And birds could no longer find the earth

Everyone went off taking in his boat
A few things soiled by the floodwaters

But now the tide is retreating
The day dawns on the prison of dreams

We will have to sew new clothes
And rebuild our vessels

Find new luggage along the way
And set off again on a long voyage

Hope for us isn't consolation
Because the person who hopes is dissatisfied

Hope doesn't make us patient
For us there's no hope but in action.

On wisdom

The wise man knows he's going to die
because everything is ephemeral
so, he withdraws from the world
he tries to forget it and to forget too
his own body.
The worker, the peasant, the employee
the ordinary man or woman,
also know they are going to die;
so they fall in love
they have children
they raise them protect them
they work, produce, create,
they come to the end of their time
and there's more wisdom in that
because contrary to the ancient sages
and mystics, who pull out of life's cycle
they don't have pretensions to attain
the absolute, the eternal, the All Embracing.
They live, struggle and die
like all living things live, struggle and die.

On means and ends

If you can't respond to force by the power of
                ideas
respond with force.
If you can't respond to violence with
                non-violence
respond with violence.
If you can't respond to lies by telling the truth
respond with a lie.
But if you do
(which is easy to avoid by sticking to principles)
take care that force, violence and lies
don't end up winning the day.

On contemplative Marxists

There are always those who know (after the event) what
should have been done.

If we had listened to them, we wouldn't be in this mess.
But when we needed them, they weren't there.
And if they'd been there,
perhaps we wouldn't have had to listen to their advice
because living by the principle which says
'only the person who does something makes a mistake'
our wise heads would
have done nothing.

There are those too whose ideas are perfect
but, like the Venus de Milo
they have no arms.

There are those who
(if you listen to their speeches
and watch what they do)
find the tree of theory green
and that of action grey.

A short history of the red flag

The red flag which in the hands of the masters
was the signal for repression and a state of emergency
seized by the workers
became the emblem
of their independence.

It appeared in the suburbs
of Revolution
at the time of the first Commune.
In 1848, on the square before the town hall,
Lamartine snatched it away just in time
to the advantage of the tricolore.
But from Canute to the Commune
it appeared everywhere
sometimes combined with the black flag of anger
on all the barricades
when the people rose up.
And from October to the Long March
it woke the Orient.

Later,
having stayed too long in the sun, rain and wind
on its pole on the façades of buildings
the red flag saw its colour fade
and ended up washed out.
(Stained by the blood of workers
it was stained too
by the blood
workers spilled.)

Tomorrow,
perhaps our flags will be of different colours.
Maybe there'll be rainbow flags
(because the fight for life
will dress itself in life's
most varied colours.)

But without the red
of living blood
in our veins,
without the red of passion
of courage and of struggle
without putting our backs into work
each step of the way,
without the power of the clenched fist
the life of the future will never be able
to win
nor find its heartbeat.

Woman and revolution (allegory)

for Patricia

I
Revolution
just like justice and reason
is a woman of strong constitution
superbly proportioned.
Quite naked under her folds
usually bare-breasted
(firm round breasts
but no question of touching).
A woman and giant
leading demonstrations
holding aloft on the blood-red horizon
of the rising sun
the scarlet banner
of rebellion.

*(In the beginning, women weren't always
invited to meetings)*

II
But Revolution isn't simply an allegory
it's a real woman
or rather thousands of women
concrete and rebellious.
Lovely plums with brown skins
or freckled white peaches.
She has a name
and thousands of names:
Marianne, Olympia, Ninon
Flora, Louise, Hubertine,
Elizabeth, Rosa, Clara
Inessa, Alexandra, Dolores or Carmela.
in 89
they were amongst those
who marched on Versailles
to make the king see reason.

In seventeen,
her feet in the snow
she stood firm against the bullets of the forces of repression.
In eighteen, in Berlin
she fell under the blows of the commandos.
Later, she appeared again
always in the front line
her rifle slung over her shoulders
in the mountains and the paddy fields.
And also in the workers' struggles
amongst the most dedicated
occupying factories
and marching in the streets.

*(Often, it's true
she looked after administration and the home...
As for true equality
that's yet to come)*

III
Once victorious
there she was, radiant and happy
full-sized on posters, in books, at the cinema
with a blue cotton scarf on her head
in her arms, a sheaf of wheat,
set-squares, chemical flasks, notebooks, babies
freely conceived and chubby.
Standing on a tractor, on the steps of the university
or sitting in the cabin of a rocket.
And still the sun rose each day.

*(In those days
you could see her in the streets too
sweeping the pavement or standing in line.
Less often it's true
on a platform or leading
a party of the State.*

*Everything was to change
with the revolution
and everything hasn't changed.*

Many yet were the battles
that needed to be fought.)

IV

Today
allegory is on the dole.
They've swept away the barricades
and dismantled the stands.
The Revolution has
grown old disgracefully
it has lost its shape and its joy
it's worn out with work.
Sometimes it has resorted to prostitution
to pay for what it lacked.
Often, also, it has been betrayed.
Now that it's put out to grass
real women are free,
free to come and go
and to offer themselves
freely on the open market
free to say what chimes with them
and to be ignored
free to be beautiful and perfect
free to shut up
free to buy, free to sell
and free to sell themselves.
(Allegory put on ice
Woman has found a home in advertising.)
And since capitalism assures the most complete liberty
there's no more need for feminism
and no more need for revolution.

(Not all women however
will listen to reason.)

V

Liberty-Equality-Fraternity
beneath the tarnished inscription appears the watchword
of this old new time:
Liberalism-Inequality-Violence.

As for the Revolution, it's reported lost.
If you're looking for it, be aware
it's lost its toga and its capital letter.
But it still runs freely in the streets.

Thoughts about happiness near a pond in summer

Sitting on the grass at the edge of the pond
taken over by swimmers
the girls, on their towels,
smoke, their breasts exposed, pale,
discovering the dawn of their bodies.
A carp leaps, a little distance from the swimmers,
no-one takes any notice.
(It's easy to imagine that humanity could live like this
permanently on holiday
but today happiness is a fleeting right.)
In the undergrowth, the light scatters, grains of rice
cast as in a dream on the floor of a church.
The girls from the beach dream of love
of the man from out of nowhere who is their destiny
risen from the dead in the midst of life's shooting-range.
The little handicapped girl, spittle on the corners of her lips,
goes by unsteadily among the couples
stretched out on their towels.
She has her arms held out, her palms upwards,
her haggard look recalling irresistibly the form
of the worst victims of Hiroshima, their flesh in ribbons.
She approaches a frightened child and takes his face
in her hands, in front of his embarrassed parents.
(Is love possible for her too?)
On the grass, the men twist into odd positions
as they drink beer.
For a moment, their dreams are cold and brilliant
as the chrome of their cars.
But already, they blur and melt
in the salt water of tears, the dull glass of weary days
spent totting up how little remains of life.
Amongst the girls from the beach
how many will find themselves
tomorrow walking blindly as dolls
amongst the debris of over expectant love?

Love isn't a chance treasure you find
in the undergrowth and which has to be jealously guarded.
Love isn't a thing but a capacity. Love, like happiness, is
something you make
the anticipation of a world where humans
from all times, disconsolate at being isolated,
can finally meet up and love one another
be together with being identical,
become one and endure, hearts and bodies
together, diving freely, joyously mingled
in recreation, the forever new play of re-creation.

I float on my back on the water sucked into the void
watching the clouds without thinking about them
as they climb sombrely in the sky.
From up there, no love ever fell.
Love rises from the earth, from the soil and from life.
Love rises and doesn't fall
like a ring in the depths among the sleeping seaweed.
Love learns to walk, step by step, side by side...

Above the pond the storm now threatens
and lightning too, but this real lightning
carries no promise.
I float on my back, levitating,
between the
green silt alive with viscous shadows
and the frozen clouds which glide on high between two waters.
Is that happiness, a silence in weightlessness, a life without
    action
a sleep where the dreams have no shape?
For a moment perhaps.
(But happiness, like love, is something we make.)

These days love goes limping,
it dreams of flying, but walks with a stick,
hobbled and deformed, it smiles all the same in the midst of the
    swimmers,
smiles at everyone, offering to all a foretaste of the happiness
    yet to be invented.

The trial of Prometheus

for Jean Marcenac

After their fall it was said
they'd sinned through pride.
Wanting to get a taste for earthly disorder
they attained heavenly order.
They'd dreamed of modifying the nature
of man and society.
They fell for the gods
which is why
they were punished in the end.
It has to be said in fact
that sometimes they made ill use
of the fire stolen from Olympus.
(No doubt they lacked a trade.)
Every poet, every seeker
and every revolutionary
is a thief of sparks
and many are burned by their own fire.
But if they gave up renouncing their gods
men would be condemned to die of cold
in the darkness.
Let the day arrive
when every creature
will be its creator.

The annoyance of revolutions

It's with good reason that wise folk
are wary of revolutions.
Revolutions are never well-behaved.
During revolutions, those at the bottom
rise to the top
and turn everything topsy-turvy.
Those who were never able to run a business
finally take over business
and in general its bad for business.
Those who knew nothing
start pushing scholars around.
Those who don't know the right way to do things
do nothing right.
The rough-and ready knock the sensitive to the floor.
High-handedness gets its way
and the fight for justice
doesn't proceed without injustice.
The river that breaks its banks churns up a lot of mud
and destroys lots of houses in its way.

But once it has passed the world is as if transfigured.
Places that had never been watered
become fertile
and no-one counts the green shoots anymore...

Recipe for the man in the street

If you like the taste of bread
you don't have to knead it yourself.
(There are so many good bakers.)
If you like good wine
you don't have to grow your own vines.
(There are so many good wine-growers.)
But if you don't like the political fare
which for so long the same chefs
have been cooking up
from the same recipes
get yourself into the kitchen
quickly.

Epode on the natural order

To hunt with a cudgel
and to dress themselves in animal skins
was natural for the cavemen.
it had always been so
and would always be so.
That there were free citizens
having the right to speak freely in the Forum
and labouring or educated slaves
over whom one could have
the right of life or death
was natural for the men of Antiquity
because that was how the City lived in harmony.
(No-one, not even the boldest minds
put it in question.)
That humanity should be eternally
divided
between lords and serfs
in conformity with divine law
was just as natural
for the man of the Middle Ages;
just as crisis and unemployment
are natural for the man of today.
Because what is, is natural.
So, the day when capitalism
is replaced
its disappearance too will appear natural.

Towards the summits

The higher you get the more things retreat
Soon the people, below, are nothing but points

*

What, down here, seemed simple to us
Seen from here, seems insurmountable

*

Your mind fixed on the aim, you pursue the ascent
(But the rumours from down here don't reach us)

*

At a certain height, the air becomes rarefied
What threatens you then, is the intoxication of pinnacles.

Reform and revolution

We're in water up to our knees
but it doesn't stop us going forward
nor from coming up with unworkable schemes.

We bail out, like anyone,
with what we've got on board
because you've got to keep your head above water.
But the level keeps rising.

(In calm and normal weather
the situation is desperate.)

But we know the damage is serious
and that we can't get out of the mess like that

(And this in truth is our only hope.)

The red sun

Above the factory road rises a red sun
(not the dirty red of bricks
but the clear, translucent red of the flesh of cherries)
a modest and courageous sun,
a working sun.
There it is in a great pale and yellow winter sky
a threatening sky which has never seen the sea
and never goes to the countryside.
And as its cold this morning
we lift our eyes towards this sun veiled by mist,
this sun which doesn't dazzle,
and we begin to experience
a feeling of fraternity for it.
(The sun which at its height or as it sets
has often been a symbol for kings and emperors
then switched to the working class
not dressed in the clothes of a star going to bed
but like someone getting up and starting his day.
Every class gets the symbols it deserves.)
At dusk too, the sun is red
says the man who finds revolutionary dawns
ending up drowned in blood.
But the red sun of revolutions
always rises in the morning.

The militant

When the sky is streaked with red
like water in which a little blood falls
when you cut yourself shaving at the sink,
at that time of the morning which belongs to
those facing firing squads in barracks and those condemned
to a life sentence of work and boredom,
he comes downstairs, pushes the door,
gets his bike and sets off,
pedalling in the dust of dawn.

He gets up
when others go to bed and goes to the factory door
when they're taking people on or on the steps
near the mouth of the metro
to sell his paper or distribute his tracts.

He gets up early
he's a trouble maker;
he attacks the indefeasible and general right
to sleep.

He doesn't always
have right on his side
but the madness of the world
won't get the better of him.

He doesn't find
his ends in himself
but in action with others
for common ends.

Whatever he does is without calculation
because he wants a world where men
and women will no longer be for sale
and where everyone will be able to take
or give
without needing to calculate.

If he gets up early
it's because the world doesn't yet
belong to those who get up early.

He gets up in the dust of dawn
to say over and over
without ever losing heart
and with the most simple words
to the lowest of the low
to those who count for nothing
that he can jam the biggest machines
and that gathered together with others
enough grains of sand can move a desert.

When the sky is tinged with red
when water mixes with the blood
of the new day which isn't yet risen
to see to it that tomorrow the world will at last belong
to those who get up early
the militant
is often up
with the lark.

Against resignation

My brother, you won't be like the stagnant water in the pond
hiding beneath the protective cover of water-lilies.

And even if everything has an end
and even if all beauty passes
and even if everything pristine gets dirty
you won't be the snow
which resigns itself to becoming slush.

To live is to refuse resignation
to live is to struggle
to try to stay upright
to hold your head high like the trees do
to lift your face to the sun
like plants and animals
it's to refuse to be the sand
they cast around
to refuse to be the dust of the roadway
people crush underfoot.

To live is to refuse to anticipate
your destiny as dust.

Life is disobedient

Who remembers the horse-tiger
the lion-monkey or the camel-giraffe?
(So many evolutionary failures…)
Nature too is allowed to make mistakes,
and for every species which adapts
how many false starts ultimately forgotten?
Nothing ever happens as expected;
secondary effects influence causes,
contradictions should resolve themselves
but reality always keeps some surprises.
'History is creative', life is disobedient.
In the order of nature as in society
the main means of transformation
isn't orthogenesis
(or breeding in a direct line)
but competition between lateral branches.
Evolution is bushy.
The weakest link will break
Lenin predicted
and the margin is in the centre.
Every great revolutionary is a disobedient militant
who hasn't agreed to follow the conclusions
of those who came before.
If Lenin had followed Plekhanov
there would have been no October.
If Mao and the Chinese communists
had followed the advice of their soviet comrades
the country wouldn't have ringed the town.
If Fidel and his companions
had been members of the Communist Party
they wouldn't have made revolution
a cockstride from the USA.
In the same way, if nature can go wrong
and correct its errors
if adaptation is never perfect,
if all living creation is perfectible

then
all hope isn't lost.
After freedom without equality
and equality without freedom
perhaps we have a go
at equality with freedom.

We are the new proletariat

In this universe where everything is always new
we are those who must be called the new proletariat
because if the old exploitation puts on
        new masks
in our very modern times old poverty is still
        as young.

We work in workshops and on building sites, behind
        machines
operated digitally: lathes, milling machines, presses
        embossing machines
we are millions, we work for bosses,
        ill-treated underlings or multinationals
but the era of industrialism being over, we
        don't exist.

Our factories have been closed; we have been freed from
        our work
but, always looking for a job, for work
        we aren't free.
As for those of us who leave school and never get
        a job nor a real wage
there's job experience at menial tasks for next to nothing
        so we're never out of work.

We are the proletarians of the post-industrial era
they tell us the computer sets us free
but we spend our days chained to ours.
Not now just our hands but our brains and
        our nerves which become extensions of the machine.

Workers, employees, unemployed or on the brink
we are the new proletariat.
In this universe where only property matters
we don't even own
our work.

We are the new proletariat.
Owning nothing, we count for nothing.
But we are the most numerous
without us nothing gets done.
And those who own everything
must reckon with us.

Psalm

Happy are those who struggle

Happy are those who know injustice (and not those who
    commit it)
Yes, happy are those who recognize exploitation, oppression
    lies
    and can give the names of those responsible
    because they can defeat them.
Happy are those who take the blows and get up again to
    fight because they aren't defeated.
Happy those who are insulted by the papers because
    they've got close to the truth and have said so.
Happy those who aren't spared by the enemy
    because they haven't been bought off and aren't yet finished.
Happy those who have no career.
Happy are those who aren't thanked, those
    who receive no gratitude or honours
    because they are still free.
Happy those who are betrayed by
    the people they battled for because from them
    you can expect nothing but pleasant surprises.
Happy are they who struggle.
(There are too many today who don't fight
    simply out of fear of defeat.
    They are defeated without having fought.)
Happy even those who are beaten after having fought
    because they, or those who come after
    can learn the lessons.
Happy those who struggle
    because they don't live in vain.
Happy are those who struggle.

On elevation

I
It's a very low world
where to rise
you have to stoop very low.

II
But it's not by copying
the low behaviour of those at the top
that those at the bottom
will rise.

III
Often you discover
among those at the bottom
more greatness
than amongst those at the top.

IV
And so hope remains and the possibility
not of a levelling down
but rather
of a levelling of the world
which at the same time might be
a raising of everyone's level.

Topology of the centre and the summit

When Flora Tristan set up her Workers' Union
she gave it a Central Committee
(where workers from all corners of the world could sit
and enjoy equal right.)

When the Paris Commune
set up its Central Committee
representatives from all
the Paris districts had a seat
in order to co-ordinate action.

Later, it often happened that a Central Committee
instead of giving a lead
gave orders.
Often, it happened that the Central Committee
instead of being at the centre
was at the top.

Once that happened the Party
turned itself into a pyramid
with a pretty large
and pretty firm base,
according to the needs of the time and place.

A time arrived all the same when
having criticised this outdated form
the centre was suppressed
but the summit remained…

To have done with this division between high and low
we should create a new party
more horizontal than vertical

which will be among the people like a fish in water
a goldfish, lively and silver scaled moving rapidly
and seductively,
able to leap
and swirl in the water.
A party which from its centre would move outwards
in concentric circles.

The people

(after a poet of the classical era)

Our weakness is our strength
and what is trodden underfoot today will rule tomorrow.
Water offers no resistance
it flows downwards and follows the gradient of the land
but it moves valleys
and breaks the most powerful dams.
Air is invisible
no-one takes any notice of it but can't live without it
and the rock can't withstand the breeze which blows incessantly.
The grass is feeble and bends its head under the wind
beneath the hooves of horses it can be crushed a thousand times
but it ends up taking over ruined palaces
cracks open monuments, wipes out dynasties
and covers common graves.
So it is with the people
most often they count for nothing, but are numberless
they occupy no position, but are everywhere
they have no power, but are all-powerful
while they speak with millions of tongues
too often they go unheard
but when they use their raw power, they overwhelm dams
when they use their breath they are articulate
if they begin to climb they stand atop embankments
grow in the heart of cities
and like blades of grass pressed close to one another
every new spring
they are reborn greener and more energetic than ever.

Of love and contradiction

The one and the other are identical
but because one is the opposite of the other
they attract
and they complement.
It's because one and the other
are different
they take such pleasure
in becoming one.
And it's because they are separate
and autonomous they can so tenderly
want
to move towards fusion.
(Towards, only...)
The one and the other are in opposition
but one and the other are linked
and in their union
and their contradiction
they transform themselves
one and the other,
they transform themselves
and one another.
After a certain time
the one changes into the other
and the one and the other
while remaining what they are
end up becoming something else
unique and different
which is in a way themselves.
A day will arrive when these sweet laws
of the dialectic of friendly contradictions
practised by lovers every day
will also govern the lives of nations.
(A possible
yet imperfect definition
of common happiness.)

What is communism?

Communism (or whatever you'd prefer to call it) is nothing
        but the common future of humanity
its possibilities written in the present as its negation and continuation,
        a seed in the earth, the spring in winter, the child in its parents;
where discord reigns, humanity will be reconciled
where war reigns, peace will prevail,
the progress of civilization resting finally
        on mutual co-operation and not on the exploitation
        and domination of the majority by a few.
Communism (or whatever it turns out to be and which will bear
        the name you care to give it or no name at all)
appears where the wealth hoarded by a few pushes life
        to the edge of the abyss, as the vital need
        for public wealth, for sharing and solidarity.
It's the end of man as a predator, a mere apprenticeship to life,
        by thinking of those who will come after.
Or where the mad power of a minority threatens everyone
communism is nothing other than the rational decision
        to embrace democracy.
Instead of a world governed by trusts, government by
        the people.
Instead of the royalty of bosses, the republic
        of co-operative producers;
the experience of self-management.
Abundance finally put to the service of a dignified life for all,
        of a simple individual and collective well-being.
Communism, at the moment of unleashing war in the heavens,
        is the decision to have done with weapons
States transformed into public administrations,
        policeman into social workers, public figures
        brought down to the level of simple delegates.
Ethics taking precedence over economics
        and politics
Communism is the people of the world
        in permanent session,
the whole world in discussions.
Communism is when nations ceasing to divide

will come together
where the north and south
will rub shoulders
when the war of the sexes will be replaced
by mutual aid;
women happy to be women, equal to men
but different,
the selfish and atomised individual feeling suddenly
greater and more willing to take part
in the development of human character.
Communism is the manual worker
becoming an intellectual
the intellectuals working with their hands
the executive the parliament
and the parliament the executive.
Communism is when the governed
become their own rulers
and when producers are at last creators.

La Fête de l'Humanité

– What is communism?
– Communism is the earth turned into a giant lawn
    full of wild flowers for a country feast, a festival of humanity
    free and peaceful;
where all the peoples of the world will be invited
    to freely share
the happiness of their specialities
with bread, wine
music
and poems, if they like.

*(Men and women of today, smiles in their thousands confetti thrown
joyously into the confusion, our fleeting and fraternal celebration –
like so many memories of a future we won't yet have forgotten – in the
middle of showers, now and again, bright spells appear.)*

In praise of friendship

To rediscover those we haven't lost
who we didn't miss
and who didn't miss us
but to rediscover them
and find how precious that is.

To exchange words that don't mean much
or to set the world to rights.
To get together under a wild vine trellis
in a precise place on the planet
to drink a glass of claret together
to swim naked under the stars.

Simply, to be there when it matters
(everybody can do that).

To listen to one another to understand one another
to talk to one another not to contradict each other
nor to confirm
but to weave a stronger net
and to go fishing in the world's troubled waters
to catch the silver fish of happiness everybody
               needs.

Friendship isn't enough to change the world;
but can the struggle to make the world more friendly
do without friendship?

On the love of absolute purity

I
Now we understand to what extent the love
of absolute purity can be murderous
because, purified, the world becomes bloodless
and many fall by the wayside.
'In the vicinity of the absolute prowls madness.'
The old man must be killed
so the new man may be born
(who never sees the light of day.)
Paradise is a place without contradiction
you can't get to
until you're dead.
What colour is purer than white?
And what colour are winding-sheets?
(The love of absolute purity is grubby.)

II
But does the danger the perfect dream
bears within itself
mean accepting mud?
Does the risk of absolute purity
make filth acceptable?

III
We have to see the dark in ourselves
and pull it into the light.
We don't fight for a world without contradictions.
We have no truck with a world
where the great silence of frozen wastes would prevail.
We want to get to the warm land
of fertile contraries.
We don't want a world of perfect men
but a world where people can always improve
hearts and bodies impure and pure
joyously alive
forming a single being
united and diverse.

When our lot finally...

When our lot finally is no longer poverty
let's spare a thought for old times
when men could hardly show their generosity
because if they didn't possess everything
they possessed nothing.
(Setting his face against the community suggested by Plato
Aristotle said: 'Only he who has can give.'
It's often those who have the least however
who give the most.)
From his beginnings man has been a sharing creature
who makes of the other another like himself
who reflects and modifies the other,
continues and completes him
because he who gives receives.
But we are living in a time
when the more property a person owns
the less they come into being...
Poor in humanity is the person who grows rich
at the expense of others
and the more humanity gains wealth this way the more it
    impoverishes itself;
– this is no mystery –
All the same only those who have can give.
(and in a society where the State is all
and owns all
the citizen is nothing and owns nothing.)
To have done with the narrow-mindedness of property
it's not property we must abolish
but poverty.
(Property has a history, its forms have evolved,
they will continue to evolve.
From the barter of animal skins or flint
to the whizzing of microwaves and messages around the world
products have evolved and become less and less tangible,
so they carry within themselves the means
to go beyond narrow property
and to achieve a new sharing.)
When our lot is no longer poverty
spare a new thought for the old times.

In praise of ignorance

If the child had to imagine
before putting one foot in front of the other
what life had in store
perhaps he would never learn to walk.
If the woodcutter had to work out
before chopping down a tree
the resistance of the air and the bark
and the wear and tear of the blade
would he raise his axe?
If peoples knew in advance
the twists and turns of history
the betrayals, the deceived hopes
and the counter-revolutions
would they ever take action?
That we don't know exactly what the future holds
is lucky for us
(and perhaps for the future too...)
– So, now you're praising ignorance?
– No, practicality.

The legend of the robin

In the rose bush a robin was concealed
   just where the bramble was revealed
In the rose bush with the pink blooms
      the red of his breast uncovered
      and by the rose bush smothered

They say he was marked
   by the blood of Christ
One story among many
Red breast flitting and calling
   close to the bramble bush

A robin lingered in the rose bush
   mischief bird
 the robin's an imp, that's the word
    sweet neighbour never heard
who arrives with a quiet hop
    and in the garden dared
    to peck the bread we'd shared.

They'd said: 'He's flown,'
   but today
   he's our own
Tomorrow will he come this way?

The gardener's lessons

I
Leaning over his rose bush the gardener with his secateurs
makes a cruel snip.
He removes all the faded flowers and prunes
the branches delicately and without malice.
Thanks to which the rose bush flowers once more.
(Here too tenderness
is mixed with a little harshness.)

II
So they'll grow and flourish, so they'll resist
as much as possible the risks of the soil and the climate
and so they'll produce more and better fruit
the gardener grafts his fruit trees.
(Because from cross-breeding comes vitality.)

III
In the plots the asparagus point to the sky
all different from one another
and all alike. So it is with men.
(Making unique and monstrous one-offs
or to go in for the production of insipid clones
are two totalitarian dreams of the gardener.)

IV
When evening falls the gardener walks his paths
and waters his plants lovingly, not like
        the rain
(indiscriminately and with indifference, as if ordered
        by a central industrial authority),
but with close attention to life's needs
avoiding the garlic to pay attention to the tomatoes or beans.
– Because nothing good is done without a little love
(something that's often been missing in this business) –

V
For a long time poets have made use of gardeners
to grow in pots the idea of wisdom
even of resignation.
(Finding serious arguments
in the darkness of slow germination
the solitary work of the seasons
whose rhythm we must respect
so that the miracle of flowering can happen once more
like that of maturation.)
But the gardener's work
doesn't resolve itself into the contemplation of his garden.
(Liberal or reformist laisser-faire inevitably
leads to the cruel disorder of untamed nature.)
Every gardener acts as an organiser of metamorphoses.

SUBSCRIBERS

Jim Aitken
EC Apling
Neil Astley
Dave Belbin
Peter Bennet
David Betteridge
Ross Bradshaw
Bill Broady
Jim Burns
Michael Chislett
Jim Clarke
Clarion Books
Ken Clay
Matt Coward
The Crab Man
David Craig
Simon Curtis
William Darmody
Jim Dry
Linda France
Mike Freeman
Cynthia Fuller
Roger Garfitt
John Green
Martin Green
Bill Greenshields
David Grove
Graham Heathcote
Stuart Hill
Stephen Horsman
Richard Kell
Rick Kemp

Tom Leonard
Margaret and Martin Levy
Christine Lindey
Jackie Litherland
Herbert Lomas
Marilyn Longstaff
John Lucas
Alex Lykiard
John Manson
SP Mitchell
Alan Morrison
Peter Mortimer
Northern District CPB
Ellen Phethean
John Pinto
Malcolm Povey
Ian Prior
Leslie Reed
Maureen Rothstein
Mike Sanders
Chris Searle
RA Softly
Don Staines
Anne Stevenson
Keith Stoddart
George Szirtes
Geoff Tomlinson
Hugh Underhill
Ruth Wallis
Boris Wild
Mike Wilson
Ken Worpole